CRAFTS
ON THE
COUNTER

Advice, ideas and designs
to help you sell your work

VALERIE JANITCH

Frederick Muller Limited
London

British Library Cataloguing in Publication data
Janitch, Valerie
  Crafts on the counter.
  1. Handicraft—Marketing
  I. Title
  745,5′068′8   HD2341

  ISBN 0-584-10374-3

First published in Great Britain in 1982
by Frederick Muller Limited, London NW2 6LE

Printed and bound in Great Britain by
Redwood Burn Limited, Trowbridge, Wiltshire

Contents

Crafts on the counter

A handbook of advice, ideas and designs to help you sell your work

Today there are more crafts with profit potential than ever before. There are the old and familiar: needlework, toy-making, cookery, knitting, crochet, pottery, basketry. . . . There are popular revivals: candle-making, decoupage, copper enamelling, corn dollies, macramé. . . . There are brand-new crafts, born of modern materials: plastic embedding, chemical glass engraving, pin-and-thread art. . . and it is now possible to dabble in areas which were previously a 'closed shop' to all but the highly skilled: spinning and weaving, jewellery, lace-making and other traditional crafts.

Step by step, each chapter begins by explaining, in simple terms, how to go about making your craftwork profitable, starting with the preliminary idea, and continuing right through to packing and selling the finished product. This general 'theory' can be applied to virtually any product with sales potential, and however specialised or unusual your craft, much of the advice and methods suggested will be applicable and of benefit. For instance, the method of costing out materials is exactly the same, whether you are making rag dolls, plastic paperweights, woolly hats or jars of chutney. The same rules for packaging and presentation apply to the majority of crafts: only the treatment differs, dictated by the nature of the item. Planning to ensure maximum sales-appeal, organising 'mass-production', selling your wares . . . the basic methods are virtually the same.

The second part of every chapter is a practical exercise to illustrate the preceding theory. A multiplication of mice demonstrate the planning behind efficient mass-production; a group of insulated bags explains how to cost out your product; home-bakes and other goodies fresh from the kitchen show that tasteful packaging makes any item even more tempting; a collection of flowery things emphasises the very special appeal of anything created individually.

Even if toy-making, needlework, cookery or flower decorations are not your own special 'thing', it is worth glancing through the practical section of each chapter, because so many of the suggestions and guide-lines are equally useful in other, quite different, fields of craftwork.

Note: Usually, for copyright reasons, designs should not be reproduced for sale (except for charity) without permission. However, in this case, the author is happy to allow any design taken from the book to be sold for profit, provided it is not manufactured commercially, and carries a label giving the name of the maker and stating 'from an original design by Valerie Janitch'.

Measurements: Whether you're a Metricated mod or an old-fashioned Imperialist – you probably prefer to use the ruler you grew up with! For that reason, all measurements are given in both Metric and Imperial form. However, do not compare the two, as they are not accurate conversions. Each design is worked out individually, to give a practical measurement which will ensure a satisfactory result: so use one method of measurement *or* the other.

In cases where depth x width are indicated – i.e. a piece of fabric 2.5 x 5cm (1 x 2in) – the *depth is shown first*.

1 A Professional Approach

The secret of success

Successful selling doesn't mean finding someone to buy your work: it means making a profit. And the secret of successful selling is summed up in the most important craft of all: *salescraft*. And the secret of salescraft? *That* can be summed up in the well-worn cliché – 'a professional approach'.

You don't need any special training or further education. A reasonable degree in common sense is much more valuable. It's all so obvious – when you stop to think about it. The tragedy is that so many enthusiastic people just *don't* stop to think. Enthusiasm is essential, of course. But you won't be reading this book if you are not enthusiastic. Nevertheless, over-enthusiasm can cause one to rush headlong into a project without careful planning . . . and that is the road to certain disaster.

In fact, a 'professional approach' is the secret of successfully marketing *any* product – on any scale. Forget about crafts for a moment. Imagine a well-known confectionary manufacturer – who wants to launch a new line in chocolate bars. . . . Putting even the smallest peanut bar on the market requires skill and experience, if it is to succeed. Our chocolate tycoon will have to sink a lot of money into manufacturing and marketing his new product – before he sells a single bar. Which means that planning every aspect of the project is absolutely vital. To help get his planning right, he will consult experts in various fields for their professional advice. He will commission consumer research to discover the latest trends in public likes and dislikes. As well as favourite flavours and ingredients, he will want to know *who* eats chocolate bars – *when* they eat them – *why* they eat them – the size, shape and thickness they prefer – and even what their mood is when they're eating them! He will probably 'test-market' one or two experimental bars, carefully judging their impact on the hungry consumer. He will investigate retailers' preferences for size, shape and price, to make sure that his new product will be prominently displayed on the counter to catch the customer's eye.

If you think all this has nothing to do with you – except as a consumer of chocolate – you are wrong! The manufacturer does as much preliminary research as possible to try to ensure he does not waste his time and money producing a chocolate bar that nobody wants. And that makes sense, whatever your line of business. . . . So no matter how small-scale your venture, you can benefit from following the example of *big* business to plan your operation in the most professional way. Just substitute whatever you plan to make – soft toy, creamy fudge, Christmas decorations or pottery duck – for the chocolate bar. Then apply the chocolate manufacturer's research questions to your own product. Which are the best-loved soft toys? What are the most popular Christmas decorations? Who buys pottery ornaments? Experiment with chocolate or coffee fudge, add walnuts, cherries, rum and raisins: which arouses the greatest enthusiasm?

You will probably learn everything you need to know about preferences for soft toys, Christmas decorations and pottery just by wandering, eagle-eyed, around one or two large stores – making notes. As for the fudge: make up a sample batch and do a test-market survey. . . . You shouldn't have any difficulty finding volunteers!

Take the *who*, *why* and *when* questions. *Who* buys soft toys? *Why* does someone feel an overwhelming desire to eat fudge? *When* do people want Christmas decorations? The answers are all pretty obvious! But they show how important it is to know your market: because knowing it will help you plan a product aimed at the most likely customer - at the time when they most want or need it. For instance, grandmothers and 'aunts' (real or adopted) are probably the softest touch for soft toys! Mothers with young families buy Christmas decorations – but the children will probably choose them. Anyone with a sweet tooth likes fudge – but older people particularly enjoy it, possibly because it is easy to handle and soft to eat. And the answer to *When*? is, almost always, Christmas or present-giving anniversaries.

Of course, there are plenty of exceptions to every rule. Having been persuaded that your potential market is grey-haired grandmothers in early December – your first customer will probably be a young bachelor in midsummer! But don't be misled. Remember, your research adds up to a statistical survey showing where to find the *biggest* market: so in the long run, you will still find that these conclusions are a more reliable basis for planning your product.

We have already test-marketed the fudge – but how about making up a sample soft toy or a few specimen Christmas decorations. This is the only way to show your standard of design and workmanship – and it is also the only way you can work out an accurate costing (both in time and money). 'Test-market' your sample by judging the reaction of anyone who sees it: note down comments, criticisms and preferences. (Try to be dispassionate: and don't consult people who will exclaim in delight at *anything*, just to please you! Their opinion is not worth having.) If you are satisfied with the results of your first 'market survey', look for the kind of shop or store which already carries good quality merchandise, and which you consider would be a suitable outlet for your own work. Then test-market your product on the buyer. This time you will not need to *ask* for an honest, dispassionate opinion: a store buyer cannot afford to give anything but a shrewd and clinical appraisal. The majority of buyers are extremely kind – even to the most unprofessional aspirants: but even if you are unlucky and get a cold reception, *don't* be discouraged – and don't let it deter you from trying elsewhere. Consider whether the unhelpful buyer offered any *constructive* criticism before throwing you out. . . . Then pick yourself up, dust yourself off, and start all over again – because the chances are that the next person you meet will be warm and sympathetic. After all, it does not pay a buyer to be hostile – because without manufacturers to supply them with stock, shops would have nothing to sell. . . . And never lose sight of the fact that *you* are a manufacturer, too (the fact that your output is small just makes it all the more exclusive!).

With a little bit of luck!

Even if a professional approach is the secret, it does not *guarantee* success: you need a bit of luck as well! So how better to begin than with a collection of lucky mascots. But before you trust to luck – apply the chocolate manufacturer's tests, and you'll find this little assortment passes with flying colours. . . . Most people want to be lucky – most of the time. And they want to wish others luck, too. It follows that there must be a ready market for lucky mascots: it is just a question of hitting on something that will be lucky for you, too! This very simple, very versatile, basic figure offers plenty of scope to attract customers of all ages and interests.

Remember though, there is more to it than just pleasing the customer: it is *profit* you're after. . . . As you read through the following chapters, you will find guidelines to help you plan a product that is not only sales-worthy – but makes a profit, too. These guidelines can be applied to almost anything, from lampshades to lollipops . . . wherever your creative talents happen to lie.

Chapter 2 explains how to plan your product. Use the mascot design to practise working out a character in the 'rough visual' form described: then answer the questionnaire, and see how you score.

Lucky mascot – basic figure

A simple design equals speedy production. Here is the proof. The lucky discovery which prompted this design is tubular velvet ribbon: a short length, plus pipe cleaners and beads, makes the basic body in record time. Add the head and hair – then dress in fancy ribbon or plain felt, developing the design as you wish. There's endless scope, as you can see. Full directions for the basic figure are followed by details showing how each character is adapted from the original.

Materials:

20cm (8in) Offray Velvet Tubing (see page 130)

2 pipe cleaners

Pressed cotton or papier-mâché ball, 2.5cm (1in) diameter

2 wooden (or alternative) beads for hands, 1cm ($\frac{3}{8}$in) diameter

2 wooden (or alternative) beads for feet, 1cm ($\frac{3}{8}$in) diameter

Small bead for nose (optional)

Knitting yarn for hair, etcetera

Flesh-coloured poster paint

Black fibre-tip pen for features (the Tempo is ideal)

All-purpose adhesive (UHU)

Cut velvet tubing and pipe cleaners as follows:

	Velvet Tubing	**Pipe Cleaner**
Arms:	6.5cm ($2\frac{1}{2}$in)	8cm (3in)*
Legs:	8cm (3in)	9.5cm ($3\frac{3}{4}$in)†
Body:	5cm (2in)	8.5cm ($3\frac{1}{2}$in)*

*Use one cleaner for arms and body

†Keep remainder to shape pointed hats

Holding the inner cord to prevent it slipping, push pipe cleaner through tubing, protruding equally at each end.

Body: Bend body in half, and glue arms between, as diagram. Bend legs as indicated. Spread a little adhesive over each bend (see arrows): leave for 5-10 minutes, then press firmly together.

Glue beads over ends of pipe cleaner, for hands and feet.

Head: Paint ball and, when dry, fit over ends of body pipe cleaner. Glue into position *only* when figure is dressed.

Hair: See individual directions.

Features: When figure is completely dressed, glue or pin bead into place for nose. Mark features with pen, following the illustrations.

Pixie

Hair: Wind double-knitting yarn evenly about four times around a 7cm ($2\frac{3}{4}$in) deep piece of card: slide off carefully and tie loosely with a single strand, or matching thread, 2.5cm (1in) from one end. Glue to top of head, the short end over the forehead and the longer loops hanging down at the back (see diagram).

Wind yarn about five times around an 8cm ($3\frac{1}{4}$in) deep

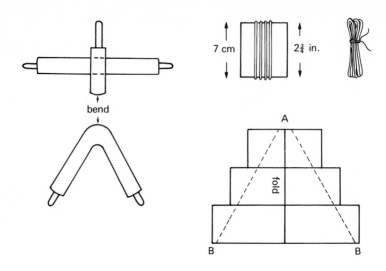

card: slide off and tie the *centre* loosely. Glue across top of head, over first piece, to cover sides. Cut loops and trim neatly.

Hat: Cut three pieces of 2.5cm (1in) wide ribbon: 10, 7.5 and 5cm (4, 3 and 2in) long. Join as diagram (oversew edges together), then fold in half across joins, right side inside, and join seam A-B, as broken lines on diagram. Trim off corners and turn to right side.

Catch remaining pipe cleaner inside, over seam. Stitch bell to point.
Glue to head (seam at back).

Belt: This is 5cm (2in) of 3mm ($\frac{1}{8}$in) wide ribbon, with a shiny sequin glued on top.

To hang: Stitch loop of thread to tip of hat.

Leprechaun

Neck ruff: Cut a 10cm (4in) length of 2.5cm (1in) wide ribbon. Fold in half lengthways: join cut ends to form a circle. Gather the double straight edge and draw up tightly round neck (before fixing head).

Hair, Hat and Belt: As pixie.

Shamrock: Cut in green paper and glue to dried grass stalk (pattern – page 17).

Gnome

Jerkin: Fringe the cut ends of a 7.5cm (3in) length of 2.5cm (1in) wide ribbon. Fold in half, slit centre of fold and fit over neck.

Hair, Hat and Belt: As pixie.

Beard: Lay a 4cm (1½in) strand of yarn along a pencil: wind yarn evenly round pencil, over centre of strand, about 8-10 times. Turn ends of strand back, and glue neatly over loops. Slide off pencil and glue round face, as illustrated.

Pipe: Glue a small wooden bead to a short length of cocktail stick. Glue into position.

Clown

Figure: Cut velvet tubing and pipe cleaners as follows:

  Arms: Add 1cm ($\frac{3}{8}$in) to basic measurements

  Legs: Add 2cm ($\frac{3}{4}$in) to basic measurements

  Body: Add 1cm ($\frac{3}{8}$in) to velvet tubing: use 7.5cm (3in) remaining from arms pipe cleaner

Collar: Join the cut ends of an 18cm (7in) length of 2.5cm (1in) wide ribbon. Gather one straight edge, and draw up tightly round neck (before fixing head).

Wrist and ankle frills: Cut a 10cm (4in) length of 2.5cm (1in) wide ribbon. Fold in half lengthways: join cut ends to form a circle. Gather the double straight edge and draw up tightly round wrist or ankle.

Hair: Wind double-knitting yarn evenly about eight times around an 8cm (3in) deep piece of card: slide off carefully and tie centre loosely with a single strand or matching thread. Glue centre to top of head, then spread out strands to cover sides and back, sticking into place. Cut loops and trim ends.

Hat: As pixie – adding a bead on top.

Witch (see page 17)

Skirt: Cut in felt. Right side inside, join straight edges below x to form centre back seam. Turn to right side. Fit on figure, and slip-stitch remainder of seam, *leaving 5mm ($\frac{1}{4}$in) open above x*: catch to body at top.

Cape: Cut in felt, fit on figure and catch top corners together at centre front of neck.

Hair: Wind double-knitting yarn evenly about five times around a 13cm (5in) deep piece of card: slide off carefully and tie centre loosely with a single strand or matching thread. Glue centre to top of head, then spread out strands to cover sides and back, sticking into place. Cut loops and trim ends.

Nose: Carve from a tiny scrap of balsa wood. Paint green and glue to face. (Or use a wooden bead.)

Hat: Cut quarter-circle in medium-weight paper: cover with felt, overlapping one straight edge about 3mm ($\frac{1}{8}$in), as broken line. Curve round into a cone to fit head, and glue overlap. Cut brim in black paper and cover top side with felt. Fit over head and glue cone on top.

Broom: Glue and tie grass seed heads around one end of a 10cm (4in) lolly stick or piece of thin garden cane, etcetera. Fit through back seam of skirt and slit front correspondingly. Glue hands to stick.

Fairy

Skirt: Join the cut ends of a 12.5cm (5in) length of 2cm ($\frac{3}{4}$in) deep lace. Gather top edge and draw up over body/legs join.

Hair: As witch – but wind yarn about *six* times around card. Glue 1cm ($\frac{1}{2}$in) daisy at centre front.

Wings: Cut in coloured paper, decorate with sequins, etcetera, and glue fold to back of figure (see page 17).

Wand: Glue daisy to 4cm ($1\frac{1}{2}$in) length of toothpick or grass stalk.

Red Indian

Tunic: Fringe the cut ends of an 8cm (3in) length of 2.5cm (1in) wide ribbon. Fold in half, slit centre of fold and fit over neck. Fix row of tiny beads at back of neck.

Hair: As fairy. Draw smoothly round to back and tie at nape of neck.

Head-dress: Fix a band of 3mm ($\frac{1}{8}$in) wide ribbon round forehead. For feathers, loop a 15cm ($5\frac{7}{8}$in) length of 3mm ($\frac{1}{8}$in) ribbon as diagram (centre loop = 4cm ($1\frac{1}{2}$in) ribbon: succeeding loops are each 1cm ($\frac{3}{8}$in) longer than previous one). Glue and pin to back of head.

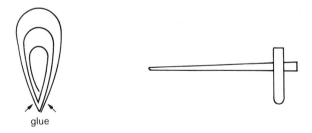

glue

Tomahawk: Cut 1.5cm ($\frac{1}{2}$in) off top of toothpick, and glue to remainder at right-angle, as illustrated.

Soldier

Figure: Cut velvet tubing and pipe cleaners as follows:

>   **Arms:** As basic measurements
>   **Legs:**   Add 2cm ($\frac{3}{4}$in) to basic measurements
>   **Body:** Add 1cm ($\frac{3}{8}$in) to velvet tubing: use 8.5cm
>   ($3\frac{1}{2}$in) remaining from arms pipe cleaner

Hair: As pixie.

Hat: Cut twice in felt. Right sides facing, oversew together, leaving lower edge open. Turn to right side and pad inside with cotton wool before gluing to head. Glue narrow braid round face for chin-strap, and make plume as for Red Indian's head-dress.

Tunic: Glue braid collar round neck, and tiny gilt beads down front. Loop narrow ribbon over shoulder and glue ends below other arm.

Gun: Colour toothpick dark brown: glue to hand and shoulder.

Constable

Hair: As pixie.

Helmet: Cut twice in felt. Right sides facing, oversew together, leaving lower edge open. Turn to right side and stitch sequin or alternative at centre front, for badge. Pad inside with cotton wool before gluing to head. Glue narrow ribbon round face for chin-strap.

Moustache: Wind yarn 4-5 times round tip of forefinger: tie loops tightly, trim. Glue to centre of face, over strap, with nose above.

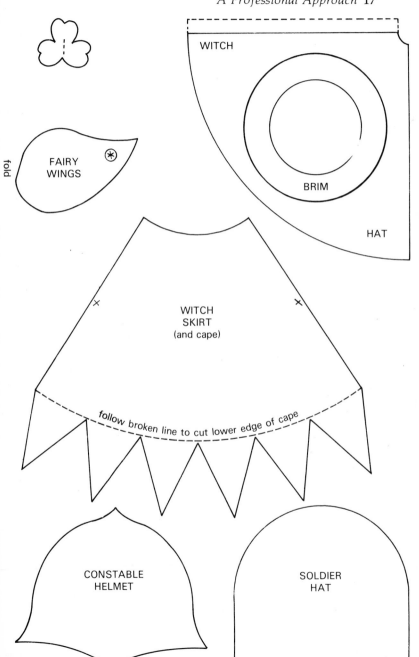

fold

FAIRY
WINGS ✽

WITCH

BRIM

HAT

WITCH
SKIRT
(and cape)

×   ×

follow broken line to cut lower edge of cape

CONSTABLE
HELMET

SOLDIER
HAT

Tunic: Glue tiny gilt beads down front and make belt as pixie. Glue 3.5cm ($1\frac{3}{8}$in) lengths of 1cm ($\frac{3}{8}$in) wide ribbon round wrists for cuffs.

Football Fan

Hair: As pixie.

Scarf: Fold 5cm (2in) of 2.5cm (1in) wide ribbon lengthways into three, and join ends around neck. Fringe the cut ends of a 12cm (5in) length of the same ribbon, then tuck through first piece and glue ends lightly to hold in place.

Rosette: Join the cut ends of an 8cm (3in) length of 1cm ($\frac{3}{8}$in) wide ribbon. Gather one edge and draw up tightly. Glue into place, with a small circle of red paper in the centre.

Hat: Use 3- or 4-ply yarn and fairly fine needles: the hat pictured is 4-ply yarn with $2\frac{3}{4}$mm (12) needles.

Cast on sufficient stitches to make a piece about 8cm (3in) wide, the number of stitches being divisible by four (i.e. 28).

First row: Knit.
Second row: Purl.
Repeat these two rows until work measures 2.5cm (1in).

Next row: Knit 2 together to end.
Next row: Purl.
Repeat these two rows once more.

Break off yarn and slip end through remaining stitches: draw up tightly. With right side inside, join side edges to form centre back seam, and turn to right side.

Cast on about 5 stitches for the brim, and knit a strip 11cm ($4\frac{1}{4}$in) long. Cast off and join ends. Fit over hat, lower edges level, and catch into place.

Pad inside with cotton wool and glue to head.

2 Planning a prototype
A question of market research

Planning is the stage which determines success or failure. So one needs all the help one can get.

We have all encountered those friendly people with pleasant smiles and clip-boards, who approach one on a busy street to enquire what kind of soap powder one uses. It may be irritating to be asked a string of questions when you are in a hurry: but these people do a valuable job for the detergent company – or the chocolate manufacturer. A similar in-depth analysis of *your* field of interest will give invaluable guidance to help plan your 'prototype'.

Your main aim is clear enough. To give the public something they want: at a price they can afford. You don't need a market research analyst to work that out. It is what we all look for when we go shopping. But it is not always so simple to discover exactly *what* the public wants. And this is where it can be enlightening to ask a few questions: not only 'What?' but 'Why?'. There are often deep, sometimes hidden, reasons underlying people's preferences: it may be some childhood memory or association, the size, shape, colour-scheme, packaging . . . or they might choose one thing instead of another simply because it is small and light, and easy to post.

To discover the kind of chocolate bar most likely to tempt the hungry public, and how much they are prepared to pay for it, our chocolate tycoon relies on market research. And since both you and he are aiming to please the customer, there's every reason why market research should work for you, too. *Whatever* you are hoping to sell, it will help to find out the reaction to your prototype – before you make a dozen. And it will probably suggest some minor (or even major) improvements which will give that dozen greater sales appeal when you *do* make them!

Before approaching an unsuspecting public, begin with a little self-cross-examination. Take a few sheets of paper and 'visualise' your finished product. It does not matter if you can't draw. In some cases, a brief description will do: but generally, if you *can* manage to doodle a very rough sketch, you will find planning is much easier when you have your 'visual' to look at. If your confidence needs boosting, use a felt pen: it will help you feel artistic! Then plan out your prototype step-by-step, visualising each stage in a series of detailed notes and diagrams. You will soon develop your own most convenient way of doing it – but the examples on page 39 show my method. (Remember, it only needs to make sense for you – no-one else has to understand it!)

Even if you are proposing to 'turn professional' with an old favourite you have made several times already, it is still worth setting the whole operation out on paper. Only in this way can you ensure it will be commercially viable. On the other hand, if your prospective product is still only an idea, you may well decide now to make up a very rough version. I always like to make something up at this stage, no matter how rough or unfinished it is. As soon as you start putting something together, you begin to spot potential disaster areas, opportunities for development – or streamlining, short-cuts, possible drawbacks, and so on. Ironing out the wrinkles now can save a lot of time and anguish later on.

This initial 'think-tank' operation is vitally important, because it is germinating a project which you hope will grow and flourish. So take your time, work at it carefully until you arrive at a pretty clear idea of how it will look, and how you plan to make it. Then ask yourself a series of questions.

First of all, ask yourself *twice*:

DOES IT HAVE SALES APPEAL?

Whatever you make must have *two* kinds of sales appeal. The obvious one is the special chemistry to infuse customers with an irresistable desire to buy it! The second kind is just as important: your merchandise only has sales appeal for *you* if it shows a profit. . . .

To discover if your prototype has the second kind of sales appeal, take a long, hard, critical look – and then answer the following:

> Is it original and eye-catching?
> Is it either attractive or practical? (If both – score double!)
> Is it easy to display on a counter or stand?
> Is it fairly straightforward to package?
> Is it compact – no bits to fall off and get lost?
> Is it comparatively* quick to make?
> Are the materials comparatively* inexpensive?

Then consider mass-production:

> Would making several-at-a-time speed output?
> Would it cut costs to make several?

And finally, ask yourself:

> Can I recruit any helping hands?

There are always those simple, but time-consuming, jobs which slow down production: sorting, preparing, cutting-out and so on. An elderly relative might welcome the opportunity to do something 'constructive'. Children usually need little encouragement to lend a helpful paw – and, tactfully organised, they can often be very useful. So take full advantage of any volunteers: but do be extravagant with your gratitude and praise – or they might not be so enthusiastic next time!

(*Compared to the price you expect to charge for it)

If the honest answer to some of the earlier questions has to be 'no', don't worry! Your product can still be sales-worthy. The whole object of this exercise is to isolate those areas which leave room for improvement. Once you have seen where changes are needed, and recognised the obstacles, you are half-way to finding a solution. It may mean re-designing an item fairly radically, to overcome the problems. But if your idea is basically good in the first place, it will be worth doing some re-thinking in order to arrive at a good end-product.

When you are satisfied that your prototype has *your* kind of sales appeal, it is time to put on your market re-searcher's hat and find out how it appeals to the vast buying public. Show people your ideas and watch their reaction. Anyone will do, from the milkman to a toddling grandson: but pay special attention to the type of person who might be likely to buy your work if it was for sale. (Since your favourite crafts probably reflect your own interests and taste – the chances are that your 'ideal customer' will be someone not unlike yourself!)

It doesn't matter if you have not yet reached a finished version of your prototype: people feel flattered to be asked for their opinion at design stage. Even better, have a selection of different variations (suggested colours, suitable materials, alternative designs – show samples and/or a rough sketch): see which they prefer. Sometimes it is the one you least expect that heads the popularity poll, and this will help you decide which has the greatest sales potential. For instance, the lucky mascots in the previous chapter offer endless scope for characterisation. Jot down suggestions for several different subjects, and ask your guineapigs to choose in order of preference.

Buy a little notebook (it's a worthwhile investment: the chocolate manufacturer pays thousands of pounds for this kind of information!). Write down *who* you asked: *what* they said: *how* they reacted: if they had any preferences: any other comments/suggestions/ideas: whether they were interested/amused/impressed: and last but not least, how honest (and therefore reliable) you think they were.

Small is beautiful – make it in miniature

Small is . . . If you are making in order to make a profit, small is quite a lot of things. Small things use smaller amounts of materials – so cost less to make. Small pieces need less sewing, gluing, are easier to handle – so take less time. Small things require smaller boxes and less packing – saving more time and money. Individually or in quantity, they need less storage and display space – and are easier to transport, dispatch or deliver. Customers are attracted to small things not only for their novelty value, or because they find them endearing, but also as a practical gift that will be easy to pack and post. So small things are big on profit potential!

One interesting statistic your market research might discover is the number of people who are fascinated by anything 'in miniature'. The popularity of dolls' houses emphasises this: you'll find keen enthusiasts aged eight to eighty!

For some inexplicable reason, there seems to be a shortage of really attractive dolls' house dolls. And those that are to be found, are very expensive. Little observations like this can prove very useful when you are on the lookout to spot lucrative gaps in a popular market! This particular piece of research led me to design a more sophisticated version of the lucky mascot in the previous chapter: a basic dolls' house doll, which can be adapted and dressed to create any kind of figure.

I developed the prototype as various characters one might expect to find in a typical turn-of-the-century miniature household. But then I felt the figures had enough charm to attract customers as a novelty in their own right, especially if one added some intriguing detail which made them complete in themselves – like the babe-in-arms or mischievous puppy. Then again, you could forget the dolls altogether . . . and make just babies or puppies: either would make an amusing tiny gift for almost any age. Always try to look beyond your current project, to see whether it suggests other possibilities.

For instance. . . . Still with a dolls' house theme, but for anyone who enjoys simple modelling, there is unlimited scope in food for the family. You don't have to be particularly artistic to produce miniature sausage rolls or a cottage loaf – especially if you have a well-illustrated cookery book to guide and inspire you!

Turn of the century collectors' pieces

For the needlecraft enthusiast, dolls are one of the most creatively rewarding things to make. They can be financially rewarding, too – as long as you keep them small. Large dolls invite all kinds of problems, from the cost of materials to shop-space for display. Not only do small dolls usually have more charm; they are easier and much quicker to make – and can often utilise left-over scraps of fabric, yarn and trimming.

They don't have to be as small as these, of course! But if you like working in miniature and can sew a fine seam, you will enjoy creating the kind of doll featured in the photograph opposite page 17. The characters shown are all intended to look attractive standing on a bookshelf, dressing table or in a display cabinet. But they are designed to the standard 1 inch-to-1 foot scale used by dolls' house enthusiasts: which means you can use the original figure (page 29) as the basis for a complete dolls' house family, of any period, adjusting the size accordingly to make children. Don't forget grandparents, aunts, uncles and cousins . . . amusing relatives give even more scope for imagination than mum and dad! If you want to make families to fit smaller dolls' houses, just scale the basic doll down to the appropriate measurement.

For you, the hidden appeal of these diminutive figures is their many time-saving qualities: tiny seams, no hems or turnings, and foam-padded bodies over limbs made from pipe cleaners threaded through a corset lace. (Usually 6 yds long, these flat laces are tubular: like the 'French knitting' you may have done as a child – when wooden cotton reels were still around!) Alternatively, unbleached or white sports laces (for track or tennis shoes, etcetera) can be tinted; whilst black laces made splendid stockings for the ladies in the photograph. Felt is a great advantage, too. Compared to fabric, it may seem expensive: but you can buy just a square if only a small amount is needed – and it is very economical in use because there is no weave to follow. It does not fray – so seams can be small and neat, and no hems or turnings are required. And finally, the range of colours available is wide and very attractive.

Heads are inexpensive cotton balls (available from craft shops – see page 129). A pot of poster paint goes a long way – so does a tube of adhesive – and hair is styled quickly and easily from oddments of knitting yarn. Features could not be simpler: positioned carefully, two dots for eyes should give all the expression needed. Always add the features last. I mark the eyes lightly in pencil first, then outline each tiny circle with a (Tempo) fibre-tip pen, before filling it in (wipe the tip frequently on a tissue to remove paint).

Proportion is the prime consideration when working to such a small scale: one flower or a piece of lace which is too large or heavy will throw everything off-balance and spoil the total effect. Hunt for the narrowest lace and tiniest beads, cut very narrow braid in *half* if possible, and so on. A new range of 3mm ($\frac{1}{8}$in) wide ribbons might have been made for miniaturists: in a wide range of lovely colours, they can be ordered by post (see page 130).

This type of doll is ideal for mass-production, even in a confined space. With careful planning, you can happily make as many as ten at a time – yet no two exactly alike. Vary colours, fabrics, styles and so on, to create a range of contrasting characters. It will make your merchandise all the more intriguing if customers are forced to choose (and there is always a chance they will find it so difficult that they decide to buy two!).

The special bonus of these tiny figures is that, although they involve quite a lot of careful, and sometimes fiddly, work – *every bit shows*! Consequently, the end-product *looks* worthy of a price which recognises the detailed workmanship which can be seen to have gone into its creation.

Check them against the questionnaire on page 21 and see how well they score. Only one question suggests problems: 'Any bits to fall off and get lost?' But this is easily overcome with secure protective packaging – and tiny bits of plastic adhesive or double-sided tape (page 93).

Dolls' house doll – basic figure

Materials:
Flesh-coloured corset lace (or alternative – as above)
4 pipe cleaners
Pressed cotton or papier mâché ball, 2.5cm (1in) diameter
Plastic foam sheet, 1cm ($\frac{3}{8}$in) thick (or wadding)
Flesh-coloured poster paint
Flesh-coloured sewing thread
Yarn for hair (see below)
3cm ($1\frac{1}{4}$in) square of felt for feet
Fibre-tip pen/s to mark features (or paints)
All-purpose adhesive (Copydex)

Body: Place two 13cm (5in) lengths of pipe cleaner side-by-side, and push one end inside the corset lace – to cover section A-B on pattern. Cut the lace to leave a fraction overlapping the pipe cleaners at A: dot a little adhesive inside, then pinch together and roll between the fingertips to form a rounded point.

Legs: Divide the uncovered pipe cleaners (B-C), and cover each one separately. Glue the overlapping frayed ends of the lace at B, and finish cut ends C as A.

Arms: Repeat with two more 13cm (5in) pipe cleaners side-by-side, this time covering them completely (D-D). Finish ends as above.

Bind the wrists tightly with matching thread.

Joining: Lay the arms on top of the pattern, *palms towards 'ground'* (see arrows): place the body on top, to determine exact position, then catch together and bind arms tightly to body.

Bust (slim figure only): Cut a 2 x 4cm ($\frac{3}{4}$ x $1\frac{1}{2}$in) piece of foam, and roll up tightly. Secure across front of body just below arm level.

Body padding: Wrap a 4cm ($1\frac{1}{2}$in) square of foam around the body (as broken lines), and oversew the edges lightly down centre back: catch top edges together over each shoulder.

Stouter figure: Wrap a 4 x 6cm ($1\frac{1}{2}$ x $2\frac{3}{8}$in) piece of foam around the body, over the first piece, fixing it in the same way.

Head: Paint ball. (If surface is rough, allow to dry *very* thoroughly, then smooth with very fine sandpaper, and paint again.)

Fit on neck to check, but do not fix until figure is dressed.

Feet: Bend up as broken line, at right angle to leg.

Cut a square of felt as pattern, for sole. Cut another square for the upper, but snip off a corner, as indicated, for ankle. Glue foot diagonally across centre of sole, then glue upper on top. Trim neatly to shape around foot, as broken line.

Clothes: White Vilene or red felt for petticoat: 8 x 12cm ($3\frac{1}{8}$ x 5in)

Felt for dress: 15.5 x 15cm ($6\frac{1}{4}$ x 6in)

(Mrs. Baker; Nursemaid; Parlourmaid)

OR Felt for bodice: 7 x 12cm ($2\frac{3}{4}$ x $4\frac{3}{4}$in)

Felt for skirt: 8.5 x 15cm ($3\frac{3}{8}$ x 6in)

(Mrs. Violet: Miss Macaroon)

Felt for shawl (Mrs. Violet)

Finely woven cotton or similar fabric for aprons (see individual dolls)

Narrow lace, braid and ribbons for collars, cuffs, caps, etcetera (see individual dolls for width and amount)

Felt, medium-weight paper and trimmings for hats

Tiny beads for buttons or jewellery

All-purpose adhesive (Copydex)

Petticoat: Oversew short edges to form centre back seam: turn to right side. Mark top edge into four, then gather. Fit on doll, pinning marked points at centre front and sides *just below waist level*: draw up evenly and secure to body at pinned points.

Skirt: Follow directions for petticoat, but draw up at natural waist level – just above top edge of petticoat.

Bodice: Cut in felt. To cut neck hole, fold along shoulders (as pattern), then fold down centre of body, across first fold: snip off tiny corner. Open out and cut centre back opening.

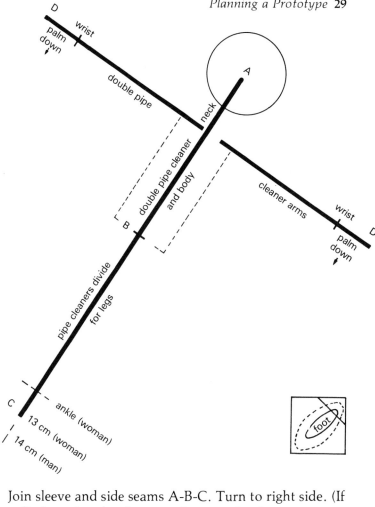

Join sleeve and side seams A-B-C. Turn to right side. (If you find turning the sleeves tedious, make these seams on the right side: but use small, neat stitches, and well-matched thread.) Fit on doll, pinning lower edge over skirt gathers. Slip-stitch back opening, then catch bodice to skirt around waist.

Gather wide sleeves around wrists.

Collars: Stitch or stick lace, braid or ribbon around neck, as illustrated. Glue on tiny beads for buttons or brooch.

Cuffs: The neatest method for lace is to glue the overlapped ends of a 3.5cm (1½in) approx. length of lace, then slip circle over sleeve and glue lower edge around wrist (see photograph).

Aprons: Cut in closely-woven fabric (7cm (2¾in) square for Mrs. Violet; 8cm (3⅛in) square for Mrs. Baker; 8 x 7cm (3⅛ x 2¾in) for nursemaid; 7 x 5cm (2¾ x 2in) for parlourmaid). Gather top edge and draw up over skirt, catching corners at each side of waist. Fix 'straps' of lace over shoulders for nursemaid, catching to form a V at centre back and front of waist. For the parlourmaid, catch the lower edge of a 2cm (¾in) square bib across the waist before adding rest of apron: then gather 14cm (5½in) lace, draw up to fit around shoulders, and glue into place.

Tie a 25cm (9in) length of ribbon around waist, and catch over gathers.

Shawl: Cut a 10cm (4in) square of paper diagonally in half for pattern to cut felt triangle. Drape around shoulders as shown, catching at waist to hold in place.

Glue head into position.

Hair: Stranded embroidery cotton produces the most realistic hair – at a price! Nowadays I make do with ordinary knitting yarn (or mending yarn, which is very fine, but more expensive). Obviously, the finer the better . . . but you can get a perfectly satisfactory result with double-knitting – as you can see from the dolls illustrated: four have double-knit hairdos, whilst Miss Macaroon has a three-ply coiffure!

The basic style is very simple. As for the lucky mascots in chapter 1, simply wind small 'skeins' of yarn around a piece of card, or your fingers. The number of times you

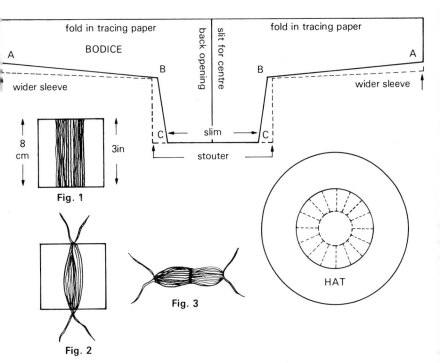

Fig. 1

Fig. 2

Fig. 3

HAT

wind it round depends on the thickness of your yarn: the thinner it is, the more times round.

Method: Wind yarn evenly around an 8cm (3in) deep card (fig. 1): about 7-8 times for double-knitting – more for finer yarns. Using a strand of the same yarn, tie the loops tightly together at each edge (fig. 2). Slide yarn off card and tie a single strand *loosely* around the centre (fig. 3).

Glue centre to top of head, then bring ends smoothly down, gluing to sides of head and knotting the ties neatly together at nape of neck.

Wind yarn a few times around a 3cm (1¼in) deep card to fill in back of head. Tie ends as previously, and slide off card – but do not tie centre. Glue neatly into place.

For buns, wind yarn several times around 2 or 3 fingertips: slide off, twist round into shape and catch together with matching yarn. Glue into position.

For front curls, wind yarn around tip of forefinger: slide off and tie tightly around centre. Spread loops out and glue to forehead.

Mrs. Violet's hat: Cut a circle of paper, with a hole in the centre – as pattern, ignoring broken lines. Glue felt to one side and trim level with outer and inner edges. Cover other side in the same way. Fold back of hat up, as illustrated, and glue to head (see page 31).

Glue one large, or 3-4 small, lace daisies (or alternative trim) over crown of head, as shown. Make a 3cm ($1\frac{1}{4}$in) wide bow in satin ribbon, and glue at back.

Flower tub: Strands of raffia are glued around a pill container filled with tiny dried flowers.

Miss Macaroon's hat: Prepare a circle of paper and cover one side as above. Cover underside and trim outer edge level – but cut only a very small hole in the centre, as broken lines, and snip the surplus felt into tiny tabs.

Cover one side of a 2cm ($\frac{3}{4}$in) diameter circle of paper for the crown. Cut a strip of paper 1 x 7.5cm ($\frac{3}{8}$ x 3in) for the sides, and cover one side. Oversew the top edge of the strip around the edge of the crown: glue overlap.

Fit carefully over brim and glue tabs up inside.

Glue trimming in front, and glue to head.

Nursemaid's cap: Fold an 11-12cm ($4\frac{1}{2}$in) length of narrow ribbon in half for streamers: fix fold to crown of head, to hang down back, and trim cut ends in an inverted V shape.

Join the cut ends of a 12cm (5in) length of 2cm ($\frac{3}{4}$in) deep lace: gather straight edge and draw up very tightly. Glue to top of head.

Parlourmaid's cap: Follow directions for nursemaid's streamers.

CALENDAR

Join the cut ends of a 10cm (4in) length of 1cm ($\frac{3}{8}$in) deep lace: gather straight edge and draw up to leave a 1cm ($\frac{3}{8}$in) diameter hole in the centre. Glue to top of head. Repeat with 7cm ($2\frac{3}{4}$in) lace, but draw up very tightly. Glue to head, in centre of first circle.

Maid's mop: Wind dishcloth yarn or soft string about 15 times around a fingertip. Slide off and, holding the loops together, glue one end of a 12cm ($4\frac{1}{2}$in) lolly stick or thin garden cane in the middle: then bind top tightly with thread.

The babe-in-arms

Designed to be cuddled by the nursemaid, the baby could also make an attractive item on its own. Add a tiny pink or blue trim – and perhaps a loop to hang.

Materials:
Pressed cotton or papier mâché ball, 2cm ($\frac{3}{4}$in) diameter
3cm ($1\frac{1}{4}$in) length of pipe cleaner
Scrap of sheet foam or wadding
White Kleenex tissue
Fabric for gown: 6cm ($2\frac{1}{2}$in) square
10cm (4in) lace, 1.5-2cm ($\frac{3}{4}$in) deep, for bonnet
6cm ($2\frac{1}{2}$in) narrow lace to trim gown
Yarn for hair
Flesh-coloured poster paint

Fibre-tip pen
All-purpose adhesive (Copydex)

Head: Push pipe cleaner into ball, and paint.

Body: Wrap a 3cm ($1\frac{1}{4}$in) deep piece of foam or wadding around pipe cleaner, and oversew edges together at centre back: bind around neck (fig. 4).
Glue tissue over foam or wadding, to cover.

Gown: Right side inside, join side edges to form centre back seam. Turn under top edge and gather. Turn to right side. Trim lower edge with lace. Fit over body and draw up tightly around neck.

Hair: Glue a few strands of yarn to top of head, the cut ends overlapping forehead. Trim to length (or wait until bonnet is in position).

Bonnet: Cut lace in two. Lap the front edge of one piece over the back edge of the other, to measure 5 x 2.5cm (2 x 1in), and stitch. Gather straight back edge and draw up tightly. Fit bonnet on head and catch front corners under chin.

Features: Mark dots for eyes – and a tiny straight line for nose (optional).

Moppet – the Pampered Pup

An amusing novelty with appeal for all ages. Quick, easy and very inexpensive to produce, Moppet could be a winner. You can cut costs even further by using scraps of left-over wool or yarn – and possibly felt, too. Shown here in silver-grey, she'd be equally alluring in black, white, cream, beige or any shade of brown: try to offer as wide a colour range as possible.

Materials:
Pressed cotton or papier mâché ball, 2cm ($\frac{3}{4}$in) diameter
Felt for body and ears: 4 x 6cm ($1\frac{5}{8}$ x $2\frac{3}{8}$in)
Thick-knit yarn
Scrap of sheet foam or wadding
Approx. 5.5cm ($2\frac{1}{4}$in) length of pipe cleaner
   (one cleaner = 3 dogs)
About 3cm ($1\frac{1}{4}$in) very narrow ribbon or coloured yarn, for bow
Poster paint to match felt and yarn

Black fibre-tip pen
All-purpose adhesive

Head: Fix ball on 3cm (1¼in) length of pipe cleaner, and paint to match felt.

Body: Cut in felt. Gather each end, as indicated, and draw up tightly, matching A-A and B-B. Turn to right side. Roll up a 2.5cm (1in) wide strip of foam and fit inside to stuff.

Position head at A, overlapping end of body, the pipe cleaner resting along top of foam (fig. 5): bring edges of felt over and slip-stitch top seam A-B: just before reaching B, insert another 3cm (1¼in) pipe cleaner as before, at B, leaving half protruding (fig. 5), then complete seam. Bend tail up.

Fold 2-3 short strands of yarn in half and catch under chin, to cover front of body. Spread adhesive over top seam and along each side to cover upper half of body: then wind yarn closely and evenly around body, from behind head, allowing extra to cover tail end. Spread adhesive lightly over tail and cover in the same way, finishing neatly at tip.

Cut strands underneath body and trim to length at each side: trim shorter at front.

Top-knot: Wind yarn 4-5 times around a fingertip: slip off

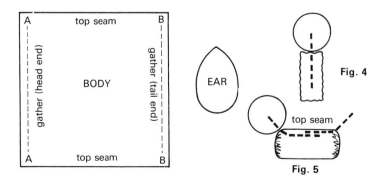

Fig. 4

Fig. 5

and bind centre tightly with thread, then cut loops and glue to top of head.

Ears: Cut in felt and glue at each side, just under top-knot.

Features: Mark dots for eyes and nose with felt pen.

Bow: Fold ribbon in three and bind centre tightly with thread. Glue to centre of top-knot.

Dolls' house fare

It is the tiny details which are the real fascination of dolls' houses. And no family who are alive and living in a dolls' house can do without that fascinating detail – food! The easiest way to bring a well-furnished dolls' house to life is to set the table for a meal . . . have the cook preparing appetising dishes in the kitchen . . . and the children enjoying high-tea in the nursery.

This opens up an exciting new field for the craft miniaturist – especially those who are already used to preparing appetising normal-size meals for a normal-size family! A special clay (available from all craft shops), which quickly dries rock hard without baking, makes it easy to model virtually any kind of dolls' house food most realistically. And because the items have so much individual charm, they are often purchased for no better reason than that! They make excellent stocking-fillers – dolls' house or no – or just an eye-catching novelty to give or keep.

Ideas are near at hand: study the variety of interesting loaves in your baker's window, as well as the attractive cakes and pastries. Note the different shapes and lovely colours of the fruit and vegetables in the greengrocer. Then, if you feel inspired, turn to your local library – for a big, fat cookery book with pages and pages of mouthwatering colour photographs! Here, and in magazines, you will find more ideas than you can cope with – together with invaluable 'artist's reference' for shape and size, and a guide to colour when you paint your 'cookery'. Use ordinary water colours, sealing with a thin varnish.

Handy hints for miniature cookery

Work on a laminated surface or a board. Read the directions on the pack carefully – especially the one about keeping the clay moist: take out only roughly the amount you need – and if it begins to dry and crack as you work, smooth a little water over the surface and then knead well.

Bread and cakes are easy items to start with – and are always in demand. You can see from the picture that loaves, bread rolls and buns are merely a matter of rolling the size and shape you want, and indenting 'cuts' with a sharp knife. Fruit cakes, sponge sandwiches, Battenbergs, Swiss rolls, jam tarts and fancy gateaux are all simple to model: just remember to work to the 1in = 1ft scale (i.e. a 9in (22.5cm) cake tin = $\frac{3}{4}$in – or 2cm).

Roll out 'pastry' very thinly, using a pencil or similar item as a rolling pin. Cut with small scissors or a sharp knife – or stamp out with the cap off a bottle, pill container or pen, and trim the edge with scissors. Use a cocktail stick or knitting needle to 'flute' the edges of flans, tarts, pies, etcetera. Dampen and seal edges just like dough, moistening with a fine paint-brush.

Dry on a sheet of foil, over a radiator or in the bottom of a cool oven.

Paint carefully, using a fine brush. Try to choose 'recipes' with interesting colour: raspberry, apricot, blackcurrant, lemon curd or treacle tarts – gooseberry flan – jam-filled sponge sandwich with strawberry icing – red and green apples, oranges, melons, bananas, etcetera.

Accurate colour-matching with a reference photograph when mixing your paints is all-important for a realistic effect. Yellow ochre is just right for light, golden sponge cakes; scarlet and crimson make excellent jam; raw sienna turns pastry a lovely golden-brown; add some burnt sienna for the well-browned tops of currant buns and crusty bread; and use burnt umber for a rich chocolate cake! Have a tube of white to mix with the above colours, as necessary: this will help to thicken up the paint if it is coating the clay too thinly, as well as making a creamier colour, for shading purposes. The tops from disposable plastic cartons are useful for mixing paints. Finish with a coat of clear varnish.

Once you have experimented with the technique, you will soon begin to develop ideas for colourful 'menus' of your own. Load 2cm ($\frac{3}{4}$in) plates with eggs, bacon, tomatoes and fried bread – or sausages, mashed potato, carrots and sprouts – or make a handsome glazed pork pie. Follow with a portion of fruit pie, an ice cream sundae or cheese and biscuits. Set smaller plates with triangular slices of toast and a heap of marmalade – a golden-brown croissant and cherry jam – a hunk of crusty French bread with a pat of deep yellow butter – or create a tasty snack of Scotch egg, tomato and cheese. Prepare individual items separately, then assemble on plate and glue into place (with UHU).

Circles of thin card make good plates – and transparent plastic tops off chemist's pill containers make useful serving dishes or fruit bowls. To make the bread basket in the photograph, fold three 25cm (10in) strands of raffia in half, and plait together: then glue neatly around the edge of a 3cm ($1\frac{1}{4}$in) diameter circle of card.

Presentation

It is not difficult to create a wide selection of very attractive food to tempt the miniature enthusiast. To emphasise its charm in the packaging and presentation, a complimentary choice of background is important. The majority of items are best mounted on thin card: if possible, cover it with a pretty gift-wrap or wallpaper off-cut, or a plain coloured paper, which will set off your wares to advantage. Look for a very softly defined flower pattern, or a 'linen-weave' effect, in an appropriate colour.

Fix each item firmly to the backing with a tiny blob of Blu-Tack or a bit of double-sided tape. Then cover closely with polythene or cling-film, folding the edges smoothly round to the back and sealing carefully. A time-saving method is to cut a small polythene bag in half down the centre: cut your card a little smaller than the half-bag, and fit it snugly into the corner, so that the two cut edges of the bag overlap the card. Fold these neatly round to the back and secure with tape.

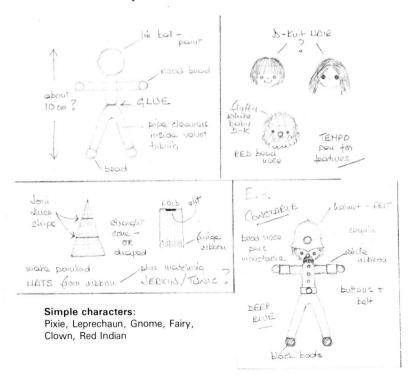

Simple characters:
Pixie, Leprechaun, Gnome, Fairy, Clown, Red Indian

3 Personality
Craftwork's secret weapon

The moment you try to sell your work, you are in competition with other manufacturers. This isn't such a bad thing: in fact, having no competition at all can be a severe disadvantage. Years ago, when Dylon Dyes were first invented, the whole concept was so new that the makers' first, and biggest, task was to establish home dyes as something the public would *want*! Nowadays we take it for granted that there is a Dylon product to dye almost anything in the home, from sheets to shoes. But if, in the early days, the Dylon people had failed to persuade shops to stock home dyes – we might never have known about them. Which goes to show that it is not always a good thing to have a product that is unique!

If your merchandise is better and more attractive than your competitor's (as you hope it will be), you will actually benefit by the comparison. And this will be your strongest weapon. For if the competition is machine-made and mass-produced – it is almost certain that *your* product will have twice as much of that mysterious chemistry called 'sales appeal' than its rival: simply because the production-line article lacks the special charm of something hand-made.

It is an old saying that imitation is the sincerest form of flattery. Have you noticed how many products claim to be that-little-bit-different and rather-better-than-the-rest, by boasting the 'personal touch'? There are hand-made chocolates, hand-baked biscuits, hand-filled lavender bags, hand-made soap, hand-painted eggs, hand-dressed dolls, hand-rolled scarves, hand-turned wooden spoons and hand-embroidered blouses. . . . Gone are the days when that famous brand of sugar declared that it was 'untouched by human hand'! Today, the human touch is a magic touch in the battle to lure the customer.

Of course, what we are really talking about is product-appeal. But 'personality' is more apt, because it sums up that quality which gives *you* such an enormous advantage over the manufactured competition. The majority of craft items have an innate charm all their own – just because they *are* individual and hand-made. Product-appeal isn't nearly so easy to achieve in something like a chocolate bar, which can manage no more than a tempting description on the wrapper. Small wonder the manufacturer has to spend hundreds of thousands of pounds on an advertising campaign to convince you that you've never experienced anything quite so thrilling as his particular combination of mouth-watering ingredients! Not so your cuddly bunny, Christmas crib – or even your bag of home-made farmhouse fudge . . . crumbly, kitchen-fresh, to melt in the mouth with a flavour that everyone knows factory-made sweets never have.

Be wily: exploit this advantage to the full. Take a shrewd look at your product. Ask yourself whether it might look more individual, more appealing, more eye-catching if you made some small addition or alteration. Personality is the expression in a lion's eyes, a rag doll's smile, the size of a rabbit's tail. . . . Even a knitted egg cosy can be individual and eye-catching if you disguise it as a winter-warm football fan!

In the search for original ideas, it is all too easy to dismiss the obvious. Those tried and trusted stand-bys of every gift counter, bazaar stall and church fete in living memory: the book-marks, pin-cushions, lavender sachets, egg cosies, tray cloths, oven mitts, aprons and pot-holders. Old, old faithfuls. . . . Why do they go on selling? Think about it. They are small, attractive, light and they are easily packed. Above all – they are *useful*: they mark books, hold pins, scent drawers, keep eggs warm, cover trays, protect hands. And a great many people know a great many more people who read books, use pins, like scented drawers, eat eggs, drink tea and prepare food. They are the ideal 'small gift' for so many people: attractive, practical – and it doesn't matter a jot if they have one or two already.

So perhaps it's a mistake to ignore the potential of these old favourites. The challenge facing one is *originality*. Can you give an old favourite a new twist? Present something in a fresh way? Change tradition? Introduce novelty? Remember, your aim is to offer the customer something which is basically the same practical item they are used to, but with a new presentation – a new personality. Pincushions are hardly original: but as long as pins are made, people will need something to stick them in. So work out an interesting design – an amusing mouse, for example, which doubles as a toy – and develop a line in your own very individual 'pin-mice'. Book-marks offer endless scope for novelty. Forget the old strip of broad ribbon or decorated card: make a 'corner-mark' instead (see page 46). Or flatten a long-legged clown between the pages, to emerge head above and feet below. Do the same thing with a long-tailed felt owl.

Do remember that your 'new twist' does not have to be a modern one. Nostalgia is big business these days. See if your product can evoke romantic memories of great-grandmama's day. Long, hot summers; cosy winter evenings; a Victorian nursery; the elegance of an Edwardian dressing-table . . . . Life in those days was far less comfortable than it is now: but in retrospect, only the good things are recalled, evoking a feeling of warmth, security and friendship. If your product can do the same thing – that is personality!

Flowers, for instance, have a language and a very special personality of their own, which ensures that flowery things have built-in product-appeal. The collection pictured on page 32 shows how a flowery theme can be adapted in completely different ways to create original designs for a variety of popular items.

The romance of flowers

Suggest the timeless beauty of a summer garden. . . . Flowers have universal appeal: they are nature's way of evoking an atmosphere of gentle calm. They can be real or artificial, lace, ribbon, embroidery, fragrant petals or printed fabric. They come in so many colourful ways to give your work a special kind of personality.

Polka-dot daisies pins-and-needles case

A new way to combine two essential sewing accessories. Use a flower-spattered fabric – like the dotted daisies illustrated – for maximum sales appeal. Two/way printed sheeting is particularly effective in this case, but any firmly woven cotton-like fabric with a small, all-over design is suitable. Or use plain fabric in light and dark shades of the same colour, and swathe the base of the cushion with a band of embroidered flower trimming.

Allowance is made for two felt 'pages' inside: if you want to include more, widen the spine spacer strip – and add the same amount to the width of fabric pieces a and b.

Materials:

Dark fabric:	a. 13 x 20cm (5 x $7\frac{1}{2}$in)
Light fabric:	b. 9cm ($3\frac{3}{4}$in) square
	c. 10cm (4in) diameter circle
	d. 11 x 9.5cm ($4\frac{3}{4}$ x $3\frac{3}{4}$in)
White felt:	9 x 15cm ($3\frac{3}{4}$ x $5\frac{3}{4}$in)

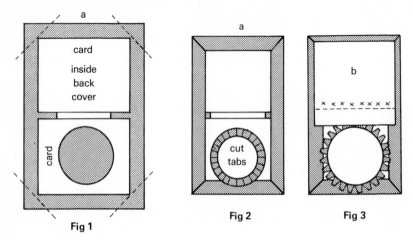

Fig 1   Fig 2   Fig 3

Stiff card: 10 x 17cm (4 x 6$\frac{1}{2}$in) – see below
Thin card: 6cm (2$\frac{1}{4}$in) diameter circle
                9 x 7.5cm (3$\frac{1}{2}$ x 2$\frac{3}{4}$in)
Kapok or alternative stuffing
All-purpose adhesive (Copydex)

Cut two pieces of stiff card 10 x 8cm (4 x 3in), and also a spacer strip 5mm x 6cm ($\frac{3}{8}$ x 2$\frac{1}{2}$in). Cut a 6cm (2$\frac{1}{2}$in) diameter hole in the centre of one piece. Place dark fabric (a) right side down, on a flat surface, with the pieces of card side-by-side on top, as fig. 1: position with spacer strip between large pieces, and fabric overlapping equally all round. Mitre corners (cut fabric as broken lines). Turn surplus fabric smoothly over edges of card and glue to top: trim away over hole.

Cut a 4.5cm (1$\frac{3}{4}$in) diameter circle in centre of fabric behind hole in card, and cut surplus into tiny tabs (see fig. 2). Turn tabs over and glue to top of card. Remove spacer strip from spine.

Stick fabric (b) over inside of back cover and spine, overlapping inside front cover slightly (fig.3).

Mark edge of fabric circle (c) equally into eight: mark card circle in same way. Gather all round edge of fabric.

Right side outside, draw up gathers evenly over edge of card, catching into place to hold: when three-quarters way round, stuff firmly, then complete. Push cushion through hole to front of case, so card circle is level with inside of front cover.

Cover remaining card with fabric (d), as above. Glue firmly to inside front cover and back of cushion.

Fold felt in half and glue (as x's – fig. 3) to inside back of case, fold level with broken line on diagram.

Scented sachets

Nothing new here. . . . Or *is* there? Tiny sachets filled with fragrant lavender or pot-pourri make such an attractive small gift that they are always popular: a set of four would be especially pretty.

They are economical to make – especially if you use left-over fabric cuttings and home-grown lavender or pot-pourri. The following time-saving directions up-date the conventional methods of turning and trimming, by completely eliminating the trickiest part. Choose light-weight, closely-woven fabrics which do not fray easily. And look for embroidered trimmings and silky dress or lampshade braids – if possible cutting them down the centre.

Note: Lavender should be hung up to dry thoroughly, then the flowers drawn off the stalks with the fingertips. Rose petals and other suitable ingredients can be combined with a special additive (available from florists or gardening departments) to make pot-pourri.

Patterns: Trace the heart shape (page 46) and cut the others from graph paper as follows:

Square:	5 x 5cm (2 x 2in)
Rectangle:	4 x 6.5cm ($1\frac{1}{2}$ x $2\frac{1}{2}$in)
Circle:	5cm (2in) diameter

Place two pieces of fabric together – right sides *outside*:

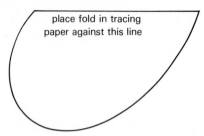

place fold in tracing
paper against this line

pin pattern on top. Cut out – adding 1cm ($\frac{3}{8}$in) all round.
Stitch firmly round edge of pattern, leaving an opening to
stuff. Un-pin pattern.

Make a small funnel from a piece of paper and fill the
sachet, then complete stitching.

Trim raw edges very neatly, fairly close to sewing line:
stitch trimming on top, or glue (with Copydex).

Add a 15cm (6in) loop of very narrow ribbon (optional)
– and perhaps a tiny bow.

Flowery corner book-marks

Prevention is better than cure, they say. So here is a novel
idea designed to stop those readers who turn down the
corner of a page to mark the place. And if *you* are a cul-
prit, too . . . they're so quick and easy to make, you can
save one for yourself!

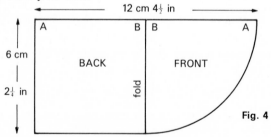

Fig. 4

Materials:
Felt: 12 x 6cm ($4\frac{1}{2}$ x $2\frac{1}{4}$in) for one
Braid, lace and/or embroidered trims (see below)
All-purpose adhesive (Copydex)

Pattern: Draw a 6cm ($2\frac{1}{4}$in) square, with a quarter-circle alongside, as fig. 4. Cut out as one piece.

Cut in felt. Fold as indicated and oversew A-B neatly. Press.

Glue trimmings into place as illustrated. These include lampshade and dress braids, purchased machine-embroidered trims, and motifs cut from heavy lace edgings.

Flower hutch wall-decoration

Most florists stock a good assortment of dried natural materials, and you can also find them in many department stores, gift and craft shops. You can even collect and grow your own. Helichrysums are particularly satisfying to grow: like multi-petalled daisies, their colours range from either cream through bright yellow to rich golden-browns – or from palest pink through mauve to deep purple. The kind of flowers you buy are often tiny heads bunched together and dyed in vivid colours, giving you the chance to plan artistic and dramatic effects. Grass-heads, oats, and other cereals can be very attractive when dyed, too.

I used balsa for the rustic frame because it's the ideal wood for a non-carpenter like me! Balsa is so soft, you cut it with a sharp craft knife, sandpaper it smooth and then glue it together. It is very quick and easy to work with, even if you have no experience of woodwork at all: but it *is* more expensive than other, hard, woods – so the choice is yours.

Materials:
Heavy card
Balsa (or alternative) wood – about 3mm ($\frac{1}{8}$in) thick (see above – and below, for measurements)
Check gingham or alternative fabric to cover: 18 x 12cm (7 x $4\frac{1}{2}$in)

Brown paper to back
Dried flowers and grasses for decoration
Self-adhesive hanger
Button polish or a light varnish or wood stain
Double-sided tape (optional)
Fine sandpaper
All-purpose adhesive (UHU)

Back: Rule a pattern on graph paper, following *inner* lines on diagram (fig. 5) – so it measures 16cm (6in) deep x 10cm ($3\frac{3}{4}$in) at the widest point, and 6cm ($2\frac{1}{4}$in) at the base. Cut in card.

Cover front of card very smoothly with fabric, cutting away corners (see pins-and-needles case page 44 – broken lines, fig. 1), and taking a 1cm ($\frac{3}{8}$in) overlap neatly round to the back and gluing into place: to achieve a really professional finish, first stick double-sided tape to the front of the card, all round the outer edge. This holds the fabric exactly in place while you trim the corners and fix the edges behind.

Wood frame:
For the sides and base, cut:
2 strips 11cm ($4\frac{1}{8}$in) long x 1cm ($\frac{3}{8}$in) wide
and add 1 strip 6cm ($2\frac{1}{4}$in) long x 1cm ($\frac{3}{8}$in) wide

For the roof, cut:
2 strips 11cm ($4\frac{1}{8}$in) long x 1.5cm ($\frac{1}{2}$in) wide

Cut a tiny piece off the end of *one* roof strip only, to correspond with the thickness of your wood.

Rub polish or stain into wood, and leave to dry.

Fit side strips against edges of covered card, with base strip in position between: shave off each end of base strip, at an angle, to fit snugly against sides (fig. 5).

Fit roof strips in position, angle top end of side pieces in the same way, to fit flush under roof (fig. 5).

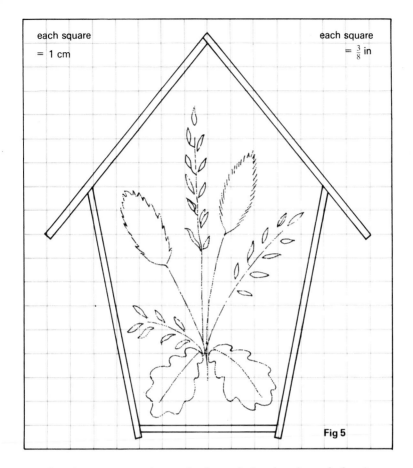

each square = 1 cm

each square = $\frac{3}{8}$ in

Fig 5

Glue frame into place, flush with back of card: begin with sides and base, then add roof, the longer strip overlapping the short one at the top (fig. 5).

Place hutch on brown paper and draw round it. Cut out shape and glue to back. Fix hanger (or wait until finished, if preferred).

Flower decoration: Arrange a few (about half-a-dozen) grass-heads, leaves, etcetera inside frame, moving them around until you have planned a satisfactory background *shape* for the flowers you intend to use in front (see diagram). When you are happy with it, stick these preliminary pieces into position, one-at-a-time, dotting a little glue on the back of the head and stalk. Then build up your background, filling in the shape with more grasses, etcetera. Break short bits off the main stalk: beware using pieces that are too large or heavy − it is much easier to keep adding than to take away.

When the background is complete, glue flower-heads on top, in the same way.

Wild oats calendar

Look out for cheap, imported woven straw table mats − round, oval or square. Then quickly turn them into artistic wall-hangings (in this case, with a few dyed grass-heads, oats and a couple of helichrysums). Add a calendar at Christmas-time, to make a seasonal gift. An attractive idea that is so quickly made, the saving on time balances the cost of the mat.

Materials:
Woven table mat (as above) − about 18cm (7in) diameter
Dried oats, grasses and flowers (see Flower Hutch − page 47)
10-15cm (4-6in) narrow ribbon to hang
All-purpose adhesive (UHU)
Small calendar and self-adhesive tape (optional)

Plan background shape, then stick pieces into place, ending with flowers, as directed for flower decoration in the flower hutch.

Fix loop of ribbon at top, and hang calendar below.

Summer garden glass paper weights

Inexpensive glass tumblers are usually quite easy to find. Discount shops often have cartons of 'seconds'; supermarkets sometimes do special offers; watch for sale-time bargains; or try Woolworth's. The two illustrated are 7.5cm (3in) high by 6cm ($2\frac{3}{8}$in) diameter, and 5.5cm ($2\frac{1}{4}$in) high by 5cm (2in) diameter.

Materials:
Glass tumbler (see above)
Dried flowers and grasses (see Flower Hutch – page 47)
Stiff card
Plasticine
Narrow braid (equal to circumference of rim of glass)
Patterned gift-wrap or plain coloured paper
Narrow clear Sellotape
All-purpose adhesive (UHU)

Place tumbler upside-down on card and draw round it. Cut out card circle to form base of paperweight.

Roll a small ball of Plasticine – about 1.5cm ($\frac{1}{2}$in) diameter for the large glass, or 1cm ($\frac{3}{8}$in) for the smaller – and press down in centre of card, flattening the base slightly: glue into position (fig. 6).

Fig. 6

fold

Push one large flower-head, or a bunch of tiny heads, down into top of Plasticine: place glass over top to check height and position are correct (see diagram). Surround with more flowers and foliage, building up the arrangement with tiny pieces massed around the central display. Keep checking throughout, to see what the flowers look like inside the glass.

When the arrangement is complete, polish the glass inside and out, then place over the top and carefully turn the whole thing upside-down. Stick Sellotape all round edge of glass so that one edge narrowly covers the rim, whilst the other extends beyond card: snip this overlap into tiny tabs, then stick them neatly down over edge of card.

Cover base with a circle of gift-wrap paper, to neaten.

Glue braid round rim of glass.

In a sea-shell

Flowers are such beautiful things, you need very little artistic flair to do beautiful things with them. Arrange them in a fascinating shell – and it is hard to fail. Unfortunately, not many shells like these are to be found on the sea-shore! But department stores, florists, craft shops, etcetera, usually have an assortment of attractive shapes, and at least one shop is specially good for this type of shell (see page 130). Do not be put off by the price of the most expensive shells (which can be *very* expensive!): the two pictured here are comparatively inexpensive types – and ideally suited to this purpose. The large shell in the photograph (pinky-mauve flowers) is a 'pink roller', and the smaller one (golden-yellow flowers) is a 'fighting conch'.

Choose an assortment of flowers and foliage which follows a definite colour scheme (never contrast more than two colours), and if possible, plan this to tone with the shell. Before buying separate bunches of flowers, grasses and so on, it is worth considering those ready-assembled collections which offer a selection of colour-matched natural materials in one box or pack. Although this is a more expensive way to buy the individual pieces, you will find that one of these – plus, perhaps a bunch of helichrysums – will fill a surprising number of shells. And the range of materials will give you the variety which a successful arrangement needs, without lots of partly used bunches left over.

Obviously this design does not conform to all the golden rules on page 21! But this problem can be overcome with careful planning. First, find your market (chapter 8). Florists, gift shops, stores and so on might be interested: make up one or two specimen shells and find out. If they *do* ask for more, ask whether they will take care of the packaging when the customer buys the arrangement. In this case, you will only need to worry about getting the product safely to the shop: a shallow super-market carton, with plenty of crumpled paper between the shells is the best answer. If travelling on public transport, don't choose the rush hour. And delay your journey if rain is forecast: a carton-load of delicate goods *and* an umbrella has a disastrous effect on the circulation in one's arms!

Before – or after – trying retail outlets, you might think about private commissions. This design makes an ideal decoration for all manner of celebrations – particularly, of course, wedding receptions. It is small enough not to occupy too much space on crowded tables, but sufficiently elegant and 'special' to measure up to the occasion. Christenings, anniversaries, official functions, dinner-dances: all kinds of celebrations are being planned all the time by all kinds of people, clubs and associations. Watch your local newspaper for coming events: then telephone the organiser, ask whether they would like your own style of very individual decoration, and offer your services. You will need to discuss how many (one per table . . . or perhaps one for each female guest?), the preferred colour-scheme (to match the decor, or the occasion, or is it un-important?), and the deadline for delivery (this is important: too early can be nearly as bad as too late). Make care-ful notes, try to sound business-like, and don't rush into naming your price. Take all the special requirements into consideration, do the necessary arithmetic, and then sub-mit your quotation (confirming it in writing when agreed). Once you have established a reputation for this kind of thing, you will find yourself being recommended, and a steady stream of bookings will result. And you will probably find you have plenty of individual requests, too: a small arrangement like this makes a charming gift for a new mother, someone in hospital, a birthday or an anniversary.

Method: Look critically at your shell, turning it this way and that – visualising the flowers inside. You will find there are two or three completely different angles to choose from: decide the best, then fill the aperture with white or toning Plasticine.

Stand the shell in the finished position to plan your arrangement. Decide the largest flower, central or focal point, first – but do not necessarily fix in place: it is usually better to build up the background and only set this in quite near the end. Follow the lines of the shell (see illustration), making sure to exploit the natural grace of each piece of foliage in just the same way as you have planned your colours so that they do not clash. Use tiny pieces, pushing them into place with tweezers (or the points of a small pair of scissors, used as tweezers).

4 Practical Mass Production
How many? How fast?

In *this* context, the term 'mass-produced' is merely a useful description borrowed from the factory floor. You won't be operating heavy machinery stamping out parts for identical manufactured articles which are sent smoothly along an automated conveyor belt, packed in giant cartons and loaded into waiting container lorries!

Applied to the kind of mini-cottage-industry *you* are planning, mass-production simply means that, instead of making *one* at a time – on average, it is quicker to make six . . . or eight . . . or ten. . . . Streamline production by doing the same operation six – or eight – or ten times over, before going on to the next stage, and you will be surprised how much time you save . . . even without a conveyor belt! More than a dozen may be quicker, but it can become very boring. It depends what you are making, of course, but generally it is wise to think twice before undertaking larger quantities: it is usually less monotonous if you split them up into small batches. (After all, this book isn't *just* about making money: it is also about enjoying what you do!)

Every housewife has plenty of experience in streamlining production – all day long. A mother doesn't wash one nappy at a time: she waits until she has a practical number. The cook doesn't measure out the flour and fat and filling for each mince pie: she rolls out her dough and makes one or two dozen. It is quicker to put two children in the tub together. And who on earth would make just one jar of jam at a time! So there's nothing new or unfamiliar about organising your work-load to speed up your productive capabilities.

To demonstrate this theme, I have chosen a versatile little stuffed mouse. He is, of course, basically a 'soft toy', and the methods described relate directly to any similar item in that category. However, the basic principles of organisation and methods for producing the mouse in multiples can be applied to the majority of craft activities, whether you throw clay pots, make toffee apples, grow bulbs or press flowers. And the rules which make the mouse such a suitable subject for multiple production, adapt equally well to a pottery jug, a Christmas tree fairy or a recipe for shortbread. The design itself is very simple: there are only three main pattern pieces, which are quickly put together – and all the shape is in the cutting. Felt is a time-saving material – and it comes in eye-catching colours to give the product maximum counter appeal. There is another important factor, too. The basic design offers opportunities to give each mouse a touch of individuality: it is left to you to decide how much or how little you wish to develop this aspect. For instance, the mouse can be all one colour – or it can be two-tone (see the bridegroom and bright orange mouse in the picture). Different fabrics line the ears, giving each one a separate personality from the rest. And if you *want* to do so, you can complete each basic mouse with a tiny accessory to make as wide a range of characters as you can dream up (you will find new ideas keep running through your mind as you sew).

If no two mice are exactly alike, it will make the display far more attractive – and the customer's choice becomes all the more intriguing. The most obvious way to make every mouse an individual is, of course, with colour. But unfortunately, this is the least practical. It wastes both time and money. Cutting the pieces to make each mouse a different colour is no great problem: it will take a little, but not much, longer. However, if you are planning to stitch the pieces together on a sewing machine – you will not want to be forever changing the spools. And secondly, unless you have hoarded a rainbow assortment of cotton reels over the years -- you will not want to buy a matching thread for each mouse, at today's prices. Nor do you want 5cm of lacing cord left over from the 20cm you will have to buy for every tail!

The multi-coloured mice in the photograph opposite page 33 are *not* an example of streamlined production: they are intended to give you some idea of the possibilities, to help you select your own colour schemes. It is better to decide on only two or three colours or colourways for your mice, so that you do not have to change the thread too often. One little trick to give the customer a wider choice is to decide on a two-tone colour scheme, then make up half with light heads and dark bodies – and the other half with dark heads and light bodies. If, for instance, you have two contrasting colour-schemes (i.e. coffee/cream and pink/plum), you can offer four variatons for your display – yet need to use only two different threads (select a toning colour which is mid-way between the two shades of your two-tone mouse, inclining slightly towards the darker).

In soft toys, ease of stuffing is another feature to watch for. Stuffing is something that cannot be hurried – but it takes even longer when there are lots of fiddly nooks and crannies and corners to be filled. Once the mouse's nose has been carefully dealt with, the rest of his head and body can be stuffed comparatively quickly, because it is easy to spread the filling out inside and push it home. Watch out for these 'hidden time-consumers', whatever you plan to do: for instance, preparing the fruit in cake-making . . . pinning out and pressing the pieces before making up knitwear. . . . If an operation takes a disproportionate length of time, it *could* make the whole project unprofitable.

Remember, it is always advisable to begin by making up a single example. This helps you work out your design, as discussed in Chapter 2, and gives you a sample to sell the idea. It also enables you to decide how to organise your multiple production. This organisation is such an individual thing that the following notes are only intended as helpful guidelines: they are the way *I* do things – but that doesn't mean they will be the best for *you*. The prototype example will give you an opportunity to plan each stage of the operation – *your* way. Have a pad beside you and make notes as you go along. Always write things down right away – in case you forget.

Just suppose you are planning some streamlined mouse production. Decide how many you are going to make. If you have an order for a dozen, you could make them all at once – or you might do two batches of six. If twenty are ordered, it will be much less tedious to divide it into two batches of ten. Multiply everything you need by 12 or 20 or the relevant number: this means working out the total area of felt you need, as well as how much lacing cord, how many scraps of ear-lining fabric, etcetera.

It helps if you have a tidy mind . . . if you are the kind of person who likes to put things into pigeon-holes. If you are not – don't panic! Just remember that the name of the game is organisation and methods: as long as you obey the rules and regulations (most of which *you* yourself will have made), you will be as efficient as any factory production line.

Become a 'container kleptomaniac'. I collect every imaginable kind of throwaway carton, pot or tray. These are your pigeon-holes. You can always dispose of them later, if you don't need them. I find margarine tubs and their lids (*very* thoroughly washed) extremely handy. Individual dessert, yogurt, cream and cottage cheese cartons are good too, as are those almost flat polystyrene

trays which come in all shapes and sizes to display super-
market pre-packed meat and greengrocery. Ice-cream
tubs, pots that have held hand or face cream, pill canisters
and their plastic tops, chocolate and stationery boxes,
polythene bags . . . think twice before throwing *anything*
in the dustbin! As you prepare your pieces, trimmings,
etcetera, sort them out into separate trays, cartons, pots
and boxes: then you can see at a glance the whole operation set out in front of you. And when you have to stop
work, it is easy to tidy the containers away without
muddling things – or, better still, just cover everything
over with a tablecloth or sheet.

For something like the mouse, cutting out is another
time-consuming operation. It would be nice to take half-a-
dozen pieces of felt and cut out six-at-a-time. Unfortunately, there are few such short cuts. With any needlework
– and especially soft toys – it is vital to the success of the
finished article that the shape of the pattern pieces is followed carefully and accurately, or the essential detail will
be lost. This means it is dangerous to cut out more than
two pieces of thin fabric at one time – whilst for felt, it is
safer to cut each piece separately in single thickness (unless
the felt is folded to instructions on the pattern). But if you
can't save time, you can economise on fabric by cutting
the *pattern* through several layers of greaseproof or tissue
paper, making sure they are securely pinned or clipped together to prevent slipping. You can save quite a lot of
fabric by inter-positioning several sets of pattern pieces
over a large area, instead of cutting only one set at a time:
this is particularly so with felt, as the patterns can be
placed in any direction without having to follow the line
of the fabric, as with woven materials.

The multiplication of mice pictured opposite page 33
should give you a clear indication of the differences between making one and a quantity (ten, in this case).

Follow their story, comparing both sets of directions to see the practical methods you can introduce to speed up production.

A multiplication of mice

Mr or Ms Mouse makes an amusing small gift: a useful pin-cushion for an adult, or an endearing children's toy. He/she also demonstrates how to organise a mini-production line turning out all of ten mice at a time! The example shows how the basic instructions for one are altered to make ten. This is a convenient working number, without becoming too monotonous: but you can convert it to any number you wish by comparing the two sets of directions to see how the amounts are multiplied, and calculating the appropriate measurements accordingly.

Materials:
To make one mouse:
Felt: 10 x 20cm (4 x 8in)
OR Head: 10 x 14cm (4 x 5½in)⎫
    Body: 8cm (3¼in) square ⎬ two-tone version
Black felt for nose: 3 x 1.5cm ($1\frac{1}{8}$ x $\frac{5}{8}$in)
Patterned fabric to line ears: 5 x 8cm (2 x 3in)
   (this amount does *not* allow for pattern matching)
15cm (6in) lacing cord for tail
2 small (5mm – ¼in) black domed sequins for eyes
Kapok or alternative stuffing
Matching and black (optional) sewing thread
Medium-weight card (cereal carton, face tissue box, etcetera)
All-purpose adhesive (Copydex)

Cutting: Cut the head, body and base once each, and the ear twice. (If making two-tone version, cut the head and ears in one felt – the body and base in contrast).

   Cut the nose once in black.

   Cut a circle of card slightly smaller than the base.

Head: Right sides together, oversew head to body, matching notches: then join straight edges of head (A-B).

Body: Join centre back seam between A and notch, leaving open below for tail: catch together again at bottom of seam.

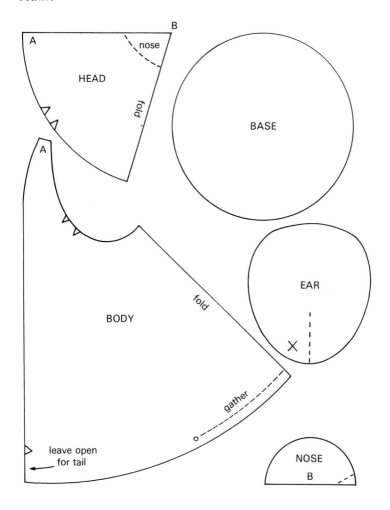

Base: Oversew round lower edge of body, leaving front open between o's. Turn to right side. Fit card circle inside and glue neatly to base.

Stuffing: Gather lower edge across front, as indicated. Push stuffing well up into nose, then fill firmly and evenly. Draw up gathers evenly to fit base: oversew body and base together, adding more stuffing just before finally closing seam. (If stuffing needs to be more evenly distributed, this can be done from outside with a long darning needle.)

Tail: Push one end of cord inside body, then catch securely in place. Touch cut end lightly with adhesive, then twist to a point between fingertips.

Nose: Glue into place, overlapping corners of straight edges underneath as indicated by broken line: push point in slightly, to give a more rounded effect.

Ears and eyes: Glue each ear to wrong side of lining fabric: when dry, trim fabric level with felt. Dot glue inside at x, then fold as broken line and pinch together. Pin an ear to side of head to determine position of first eye: mark second to correspond. Stitch on sequins, using black thread, beginning and ending behind ears. (Eyes may be glued and applied with tweezers or a pin, if preferred.)

Glue ears into place.

Materials:

To make ten mice:
Felt: 25cm ($\frac{1}{4}$yd) 90cm (36in) wide
OR half above amount in each shade for two-tone version
Black felt for nose: 7.5 x 6cm (3 x $2\frac{1}{4}$in)
Patterned fabric to line ears: 5 x 8cm (2 x 3in) for *each* mouse (this amount does *not* allow for pattern matching)
1.50m ($1\frac{3}{4}$yd) lacing cord for tail

20 small (5mm-$\frac{1}{4}$in) black domed sequins for eyes
Kapok or alternative stuffing
Matching and black (optional) sewing thread
Medium-weight card (cereal carton, face tissue box etcetera)
All-purpose adhesive (Copydex)

Cutting: Cut the head, body and base ten times each: if making two-tone mice, cut five pieces in each shade. Cut the ear twenty times (or ten in each shade). Place heads, bodies, bases and ears in four separate containers – dividing further into colours, for two-tone versions.

Cut ten black noses. Place in a small container, and set aside.

Cut ten circles of card slightly smaller than the base. Stack in another container.

First stage: Right sides together, oversew each head to a body, matching notches (stitching contrasting felts together for two-tone version): join straight edges of head (A-B).

Join centre back seam between A and notch, leaving open below for tail: catch together at bottom of seam.

Oversew base round lower edge of body, leaving front open between o's.

As each piece is completed, place together to form a new heap.

Second stage: Turn each piece to right side. Fit card circle inside and glue neatly to base.

Third stage: Gather lower edge of body between o's. Stuff each shape firmly and evenly, pushing well up into nose. Draw up gathers evenly to fit base: oversew together, adding more stuffing just before finally closing seam. (If stuffing needs to be distributed more evenly, this can be done from outside with a long darning needle.)

Fourth stage: Push end of cord through gap at base of back seam, and catch securely into place. Measure 14.5cm (5¾in) for tail, and cut cord: touch *both* cut ends lightly with adhesive to prevent fraying, then twist each to a point between fingertips. Repeat for remaining mice.

Fifth stage: Glue noses into place, overlapping corners of straight edges underneath, as indicated by broken line. Push point in slightly to give a more rounded effect.

Sixth stage: Glue each pair of ears to wrong side of lining fabric: when dry, trim fabric level with felt. Dot glue inside at x, then fold as broken line, and pinch together.

Seventh stage: Pin an ear to side of head to determine position of first eye, matching ears to head for two-tone version: mark second eye to correspond. Stitch on sequins, using black thread, beginning and ending behind ears. (Eyes may be glued and applied with tweezers or a pin, if preferred.)

Eighth stage: Glue ears into place.

The more mice the merrier – individual characterisation

Turning your basic mouse into an endearing little person-ality costs a bit more time and thought – but it makes him or her a lot more special, and could mean a handsome increase in profit.

Bridal mice
Groom: Two-tone mouse in dark and silver grey, wears a jaunty bow-tie made from 7cm (2¾in) spotted ribbon, 1.5cm (⅝in) wide. Fold the cut ends under so they overlap at centre, then gather centre tightly and bind with a narrow strip of ribbon.

The brim of his smart topper is black paper covered

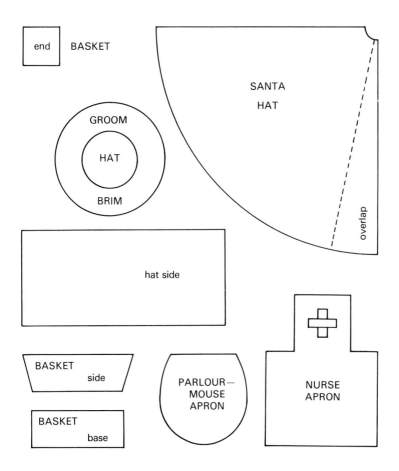

with felt. Cut the side in medium-weight paper, as pattern. Roll into a cylinder and fit into hole in brim: allow to open out, and mark overlap. Remove and cover with black felt, *omitting overlap*. Roll up and glue overlap. Glue carefully on top of brim. Cut a circle of paper to size for crown, cover with felt and glue to top of hat. Fold up brim and glue to hold. Glue hat to head, as illustrated.

Bride: 35cm (14in) of 2cm ($\frac{3}{4}$in) wide lace is folded in half for her veil, the straight edges narrowly overlapped and joined, drawing up stitches to gather centre of lace at top of veil. Attach to top of head, adding a lacy motif, if liked.

Her posy is a flower-embroidered lace motif, with a length of very narrow ribbon folded behind.

Bridesmaid mouse: Her head-dress is a 30cm (12in) length of very narrow ribbon: mark eight 1.5cm ($\frac{5}{8}$in) wide sections at the centre, then catch marked points tightly together to form loops. Fix to top of head, as illustrated.

Market-mouse:

Her 10cm (4in) square shawl of lightweight fabric has threads drawn to form a fringe.

Her basket is cut from very thin balsa wood (or card), then glued together, with a handle of raffia (or coloured paper).

Parlour-mouse

Her cap is a 2.5cm (1in) diameter lace motif. The edge is cut from a similar motif and glued round her apron. (Nothing was wasted: the central daisy topped the bride's veil.) 30cm (12in) very narrow ribbon makes the waistband and ties (glue apron on first).

Santa-mouse

Cut his hat in red felt. Curve round into a cone and glue overlap. Glue cotton wool around lower edge, and roll a tiny ball for pom-pon. Fix a short length of pipe cleaner inside, reaching up into point, then bend top half over, as illustrated. Pad lightly with cotton wool before fixing to head.

His whiskers are more cotton wool, lightly glued into place.

Red-cross-mouse
A 6cm (2¼in) length of 1.2cm (½in) wide ribbon makes her cap, the overlapping cut ends glued together.

Her apron is cut in firmly-woven white cotton.

The red crosses are made from a narrow strip of coloured paper (or ribbon), and glued on afterwards.

Muffler-mouse
His answer to winter chills could equally well be a colourful length of woven braid. But in this case, it did not take long to knit 5 stitches in 'random' shaded yarn, on fairly fine needles, to make a 20cm (8in) long striped scarf. Knot securely round neck.

Harvest-mouse
His coat is a warm shade of soft brown felt and he carries an ear of grain to remind him of the field he calls home sweet home!

5 Getting the price right
Count-down to profit

The right price is the one which allows you a satisfactory margin of profit – without pricing your product out of the market place. This means you have to find a happy medium between under-charging and over-pricing your work. How to arrive at this figure is a question about which craftspeople are often anxious and confused: and it is the most difficult one to answer, because everyone is an individual. How experienced you are; how fast; how highly you value your talents, your time and so on. It is impossible to lay down any set rules and regulations, because it is such a personal thing, depending on how much you put *into* your work, and how much you expect to get *out* of it. Fortunately, the other factor – the cost of materials – is easier to calculate: though even when you have counted up how much you actually spent, you must not forget the hidden overheads.

Much depends on your particular craft, too. A slow output doesn't necessarily mean you are a slow worker. Patchwork quilts, for instance, were not meant to be finished in an evening. This is why it is necessary to assess your own work, and your own attitude to it, in order to arrive at a satisfactory 'pricing policy' for *you*. For instance, if patchwork happens to be your thing, you may come to the conclusion that it is a better bet commercially to produce several beautiful patchwork cushions than one exquisite patchwork quilt. Patch-for-patch, the price of the cushions will work out more expensive than the quilt, but you will probably find more people who can afford a cushion than are able to splash out for a full-size bedspread. (If you have set your heart on selling a quilt, it is wiser to work only to special commissions.)

Your two main 'ingredients' are *materials* and *labour*. Have a cash book in which to record everything you buy: keep a separate page for each job, and enter every item, the moment you get home – or when you un-pack. Other ingredients you mustn't forget are travelling expenses, telephone calls and postage, experimental materials, special equipment, packing . . . and any additional extras which might crop up. As individual items, some of these may be only a few pence, but the pennies soon mount up, so be sure to jot down every single small sum. Don't forget the 'petty cash' too – all those unavoidable expenses like stationery, fares and so on, which do not always relate to any specific job. It is best to list these separately, so that you can total them over a period and add a percentage when costing out. After all, the whole object of the exercise is to find out if you are going to make a profit: so it's essential to adopt that thoroughly professional attitude, and get your sums right!

It is all too easy, in a mood of happy enthusiasm, to under-price your product – either by forgetting to add in every single penny spent on materials plus 'overheads', or by mis-judging the amount of time it takes to make. For instance, when you have to deliver the finished product, remember to add on the time and money spent on this part of your service. If you want to avoid burning the midnight oil merely to cover your costs, you can see how important it is to be quite sure you have allowed for *everything*, including your time (all those other tasks, as well as actual labour), before you arrive at the amount you consider would give you an adequate return.

Only *you* can decide how much your time is worth. But the best way to find a basis on which to estimate, is to keep a time-sheet. Have a piece of paper and a pencil handy alongside your work, so that you can't forget to fill it in. Divide the sheet into three columns. Enter the *date* in the first column. In the second, the *time when you start work*. Then, when you finish, enter the *time worked* in the last column: for instance, if you started at 2 p.m. and stopped at 5.15 – fill in $3\frac{1}{4}$ hours. Then, at the end of the job, all you have to do is total the number of hours in the third column.

However, having done all that . . . deciding what your time is worth is the really tough part. Because if you value your time at a rate comparable with an office job, or serving in a shop, your work will almost certainly be too highly priced to be competitive. This is the major disadvantage of doing craftwork at home – and it is something which has to be recognised and accepted at the outset. However, there *are* compensations: enjoying what you do is one of them!

If you start working out the cost of light, heat, telephone rental, wear-and-tear on your sewing machine – plus the electricity it consumes – paperwork and cups of tea to keep you going . . . you'll probably end up with a nervous breakdown instead of a profit. Nevertheless, all these things *are* unavoidable outgoings, and unless you decide to subsidise your craftwork (which is not very business-like), these items will have to be paid for out of your profit. But unless you positively enjoy mathematical calculations, it is probably better to decide an amount which you treat as a 'kitty' to cover all these overheads, and add a percentage to each job, along with your petty cash allowance. In time you will discover whether you are over- or under-estimating your overheads, and adjust accordingly.

This is the moment of truth. . . . Add everything up and then divide by the number of articles you expect to produce. Now! Are you sure the price that emerges is practical? Don't forget that, if you are supplying a retailer, the figure you arrive at is not the one that will be on the price tag in the shop. The store will add their 'mark-up' – a sizeable percentage to allow for their own overheads and profit. The amount varies from shop to shop, so you must take this into consideration to 'guesstimate' the price at which it will be offered to the customer.

This brings us to another aspect of the professional approach to pricing: being competitive. Have you assessed the competition? And do you measure up to it? This doesn't mean you have to undercut every other cuddly bunny on the market: but it does mean your bunny will not stand much of a chance if it is twice the price of similar stuffed rabbits! It is time for some more market research – so out with the pencil and notebook again. Visit any shop which sells the type of thing you are planning to produce, and assess the competition, making careful note of the prices – *and* quality.

Now compare your own price. If it does not compare favourably – ask yourself why. The quality of workmanship in your own hand-made product ought to be superior to manufactured goods: this is the most important inducement you have to offer. And you will probably have used better-quality materials. Cast a coldly critical eye over your creation – and see where you might save. . . . A different fabric? A less expensive trimming – or less of it? Narrower lace? Nylon ribbon instead of satin? Felt accessories instead of suede? Give every question thoughtful consideration – but do take care not to go over the top.

Cutting your outlay on materials to a minimum is the sure way to a healthy profit margin. But *too much* penny-pinching – especially on quality – can 'spoil the ship for a ha'p'orth of tar', as Grandma used to say! Shoddy materials can only result in a shoddy product, no matter how much skill and care you have lavished on it. Whereas just a scrap of fancy trimming, a touch of interesting decoration, or a specially nice fabric, will lift it into the 'luxury' class – probably with much less time-consuming effort on your part, too. The high standards you set yourself are worthy of good materials. So try to economise only so far as to streamline your product, cutting out any unnecessary features, but retaining the quality and good taste which reflect and emphasise your own skilled craftsmanship. Don't worry if your product costs a little more than the others: just make sure it is worth the extra – and make sure it shows.

What about time? The other way to save is to cut down, or better still, cut out, any time-consuming operations, so that you can increase productivity. Go right back to the beginning and probe every stage, in an attempt to streamline production. Ask yourself searching questions – and be sure to give honest replies.

This critical appraisal of your own work is the hardest part of the whole operation – especially if it involves much butchery of your lovingly created work of art! But grit your teeth, remember you are a Tough Professional in a Hard World – and try to be as dispassionate as possible. (A good device is to pretend it's someone else's work: preferably that of your worst enemy!)

One great time-saver for most needlecrafts comes in a tube: *fabric adhesive* is the instant substitute for much tedious sewing. **Never stitch what you can stick!**

After glue, the next great time-saver is simplicity. Take an imaginary pruning knife to your product – and SIMPLIFY! Cut out any unnecessary seams, trimmings and decoration: it is surprising how often one finds a thing is not only cheaper to make, but is actually *improved* by the removal of fiddly detail. Simplification and substitution, if handled with care, need not diminish the product in any way.

Remember the chocolate bar research? Suppose the

makers had devised a splendid confection of crushed honeycomb and almonds in caramel, thickly coated with chocolate. Everyone loved it – but the price came out at double that of any other bar. . . . The next stage would be to adapt the prototype, to produce a *similar* bar at a more acceptable price. Peanuts instead of almonds . . . honeycomb replaced by crispy rice . . . air whipped into the caramel to double the volume . . . and a thinner chocolate coating. The new bar retains all the nutty, crunchy, chewy qualities of the original, but the cost is cut dramatically.

It may seem hard, but if your prototype is to be commercial – it must have the chocolate bar treatment. A practical reassessment without loss of quality. Once you have taken the plunge, you will not find it as bad as you expect – and you may end up with a better product. But be warned: even when you've been doing it for years, it doesn't get any easier!

Costing out an item

The insulated bags featured in the second part of this chapter provide a simple exercise in pricing. The following example shows how to estimate the amount of money and time you spend on the bags, plus the other allowances. If, when you have worked out your 'cost' figure, you can add a profit margin of thirty-three per cent and still have a competitive product, you should feel satisfied.

> . . . cm fabric @ £ . . . . per metre:
> . . . cm ribbon @ . . . . p. per metre:
> Size . . . . padded envelope:
> Sewing threads:
> Fares, 'phone calls and other incidentals:
> Percentage towards overheads/petty cash:

When you plan to make several identical bags, add up the total amount you will need to buy of each item, and then divide by the number of bags you intend making.

Now estimate . . .
> Time allowed for planning and development:
> Time allowed for shopping materials:
> Time allowed for making bags:
> Time allowed for packing and delivery:

It is up to you to decide how much your time is worth –
and then revise it to arrive at a more realistic figure!
Sadly, if you draw comparisons with the hourly rate for
an office job, your work will nearly always be too highly
priced to be competitive. This is why you *must* enjoy your
craft, and like working at home – otherwise it isn't worth
doing: there are more lucrative ways to increase your
income.

It's in the bag!

A shopping bag is always useful . . . but these smartly
striped examples have a hidden secret. Each has a padded
envelope with insulating qualities fitted inside to help keep
hot foods warm and cold things cool – in transit from
shop to home. They're ideal for picnics, too, and for a
packed lunch at school or work. If the lining become
soiled, it is easily replaced with a fresh envelope. There is
a good range of sizes, based on the standard postal
envelope measurements, and they're all decorated with
eye-catching ribbons. The larger bags – for carrying meat,
fish, frozen foods and vegetables, ice-cream or takeaway
meals – are designed so that the top can be folded down
under the handles. The smallest are simply pockets – per-
fect for slipping into the shopping basket ready to protect
a packet of butter or a carton of cream.

Use denim or a heavy poplin to make the bags with their
self fabric handles. The insulated linings are padded
envelopes or 'Jiffybags', which are available from all good
stationers. Specific measurements are not given in the
directions, as you will want to plan these to fit your own

choice of envelope size.

Materials:
Firm fabric (see above)
Padded envelope or Jiffybag
Grosgrain or embroidered ribbon to trim
Matching sewing threads

If possible, cut the fabric in one piece – folding around the base of the envelope. For the larger bags, use the width of the fabric for the length of the bag, so that the selvedges form the top edges – turning any surplus inside to form the top hem. Allow about 2.5cm (1in) at each side (making the fabric at least 5cm (2in) wider than the envelope). For the smaller bags, where the width of the fabric does not determine the depth of the top hem, allow about 5cm (2in) from *just above* the edge of the envelope.

For the handles, cut a strip of fabric, 5cm (2in) wide, long enough to make two handles (ideally, use the width of the fabric again: make in one long strip, and cut in half when finished).

Fold the fabric around the envelope, and turn the top hem under, to determine position of ribbon trim. Make the top horizontal band (under which the handles are fixed) about 12-13cm (5in) below the top edge of the bag. Pin ribbon into place, on both sides of bag, and then stitch neatly, *leaving upper edge of top horizontal band unstitched*.

Stitch top hem neatly.

Fold the raw edges of the handle strip so that they meet at the centre, wrong side inside: then fold in half, raw edges inside, and stitch close to double folded edge. Cut in half and stitch a handle securely at each side, under ribbon. Then stitch down top edge of ribbon, over handles.

Right side inside, stitch side seams firmly, back-stitching at top. Turn to right side and fit envelope inside.

6 Seasonal trends
Supplying a demand

Christmas comes but once a year: and when it comes, it brings good cheer. It also brings a bonanza for the shops and stores, as well as providing an excuse for all those fund-raising sales of work which appear in profusion towards the year's end. Anticipating this unparalleled buying and spending spree, store buyers are busily planning their gift counters as early as the previous January or February.

Needless to say, the Christmas season is a gift to the majority of craftspeople. Of course, if you happen to specialise in running up two-piece swimsuits or freezing fruity ice lollies, your share of the Christmas trade will be minimal: but then you'll enjoy *your* season of good cheer in the summer!

But this chapter is not *all* about Christmas. It is about planning your merchandise to meet a demand – whatever that demand might be. It could be Valentine cards, Easter bonnets, birthday cakes, the holiday trade or Passover. Nevertheless, Christmas is still the most important sales period of the year: so it is essential to consider all the possibilities it offers everyone who is into crafts. If, like the swimsuit supplier, your merchandise is simply not right for the Christmas trade, then you will be equally keen to find suitable outlets at the appropriate season when your work *is* in demand. It's still worth considering the possibility of trying other things too. A good cook, living in a picturesque village, might make strawberry jam and scones – to delight holidaymakers with her country garden cream teas. But she won't put her feet up in the winter until she has discovered an outlet for her sausage rolls and mince pies. The nearby pub might be pleased to be able to offer customers tasty snacks with their drinks: or she could supply home-made refreshments to order, for local meetings and functions.

Mince pies bring us smartly back to the inevitable Christmas again: which goes to prove it is almost *never* too early to start thinking about it. Even while you are stuffing soft toys or knitting baby clothes for summer fetes, you can give a thought to plans for the Christmas bazaar. And if you wait until October or November to approach shops, you will find that you are too late!

If you are reading this in the period leading up to Christmas – take heart: you couldn't have chosen a better time. Although you won't be able to take advantage of *this* year's festive spirit, you are in an ideal position to *observe* – and prepare yourself to get in with a head start next year. Haunt the gift, toy and decoration departments – wherever your own interests lie – and watch what customers buy. See what people select from the choice available. Do you think they are influenced by price; by size; by volume; by colour; or by tasteful design? Jot down everything you notice and every conclusion you draw. Make a general study, not just of articles directly in competition with your own. Pretend you are a student of human psychology! That hairy young man with the unruly black beard: he's a proud father buying a blue Teddy Bear for his son's first Christmas present. The elderly lady is choosing a jig-saw puzzle for her grandson – because she doesn't approve of guns.

All these glimpses of human nature provide valuable material when you start to think out your own Christmas plan of campaign. An alternative pink/blue ribbon 'identity tag' could be an original idea for any soft toy suitable for a new baby. Items suggesting World War III or criminal violence might go down well with small boys, but they may not be so popular with those who hold the purse-strings. . . . Always remember that while it is necessary, ultimately, to appeal to the recipient – the givers are the people whose attention you must catch in the first place: it's *their* money you are after!

For those whose speciality is in the kitchen, seasonal trends are very important, whether dictated by nature or traditional demands. Jams, jellies and preserves all *have* to be made in the summer, followed by chutney and pickles in the autumn. Christmas means a call for mincemeat and Dundee cakes, marzipan animals and glacé fruit. So many of our eating habits are traditional that the cook has only to look at the calendar to know what ingredients are available, and what goodies to prepare.

If your talents lie with the needle or more general crafts, these pre-Christmas observations will help to jog your memory when you are making gifts and decorations in a heatwave the following July. For instance, your jottings may remind you that the most popular Christmas decorations are fairly small and easy to handle: ideally they should be adaptable, so that they can be used for more than one purpose: i.e. hanging on a tree, standing on a table or attached to a gift. And, unless you have a really earth-shattering gimmick, it's safer to stay with the traditional themes – trying to ring the changes in an original way on Santas and snowmen; reindeer and sleighs; angels and fairies; holly and mistletoe; robins and snowflakes.

Make a careful note of any ideas which suggest themselves during your 'research' periods. Try to elaborate on them while the original stimulus is still fresh in your mind: then you can safely put away your detailed notes until you are ready to develop the design to a more finished stage. Treat your project in the usual way – developing a prototype to work out the best method of production, as well as to use for demonstration purposes when discussing the design with potential buyers. Never make up quantities of a decoration or gift item until you have secured a firm order: often a buyer may like a design – but will want some small detail handled differently.

The Christmas decorations on page 81 illustrate some practical design ideas, all of which follow the guidelines mentioned above. They are fairly small and compact, adaptable and based on traditional themes. They are also inexpensive to produce, and comparatively quick, especially when made in quantity.

Making the most of Christmas
Santa Claus tree trims

This versatile little decoration is quick and easy to make, especially in quantity. Apart from hanging on the tree, it could decorate a special gift . . . or rest on the Christmas dinner-table – perhaps one for each guest.

For a quality product, cut the hat and whiskers in felt: for something less durable, but cheaper, use cartridge-weight paper

Materials:
Thin card (cereal carton, etcetera)
Flesh-coloured cartridge paper
Coloured felt: 12 x 6cm (5 x $2\frac{1}{2}$in)
White felt: 10 x 6.5cm (4 x $2\frac{1}{2}$in)
Cotton wool (optional)
20cm (8in) strong thread or fine cord to hang
Black and red fibre-tip pens
All-purpose adhesive (mainly Copydex)

Draw a 5cm (2in) diameter circle on pink paper: glue to card and cut out.

Draw a similar circle on tracing paper: place over pattern, matching broken lines. Using a soft pencil, carefully trace eyes, nose and lower edge of hat.

Turn tracing over, then place face down over pink circle and draw over eyes, nose and hat edge with the same pencil, pressing firmly so that an impression remains when the paper is removed. Turn paper over and repeat for each new face. Ink in eyes and nose neatly, with fibre-tip pens.

Trace off separate patterns for the hat (following broken lines *to lower edge of band*), the band, beard and moustache. Trace another pattern for the hat back, this time following head circle for the lower edge, as indicated.

Cut the two hat pieces in coloured felt, and the rest in white: the beard (using pinking shears for curved edge) and moustache once each, and the band twice.

Glue front hat to face, lower edge level with marked line. Glue one band over lower edge. Turn head over and glue second hat piece to back: turn second band upside-down and glue over lower edge of hat back.

Glue beard into position. To give fluffy appearance, tease out cotton wool to cover felt: cut straight across top, then tear to shape of beard. Glue along top edge only. Glue moustache on top. (UHU is best for this.)

Knot a loop of thread through point of hat, then glue a 1cm ($\frac{3}{8}$in) diameter circle of white felt to tip.

Cheery snowmen – for table or tree

Make the larger size as an individual decoration for each place setting on the festive table. The smaller ones have a loop – to hang from the Christmas tree.

To cut costs, the felt can be omitted: but the finished result will not be so effective.

Large snowman

Materials:
White cartridge-weight paper: 10 x 30cm (4 x 12in)
Stiff black paper: 6cm ($2\frac{1}{4}$in) diameter circle
Medium-weight black paper: 2.5 x 14cm (1 x $5\frac{1}{2}$in) and a
    4cm ($1\frac{1}{2}$in) diameter circle
White felt: 7.5 x 14cm (3 x $5\frac{1}{2}$in)
25cm (10in) ribbon, 2.5cm (1in) wide, for scarf
15cm (6in) ribbon, 1.5cm ($\frac{1}{2}$in) wide, for hat-band
Small wooden bead for nose (about 5mm diameter)
Tiny black self-adhesive labels (about 5mm diameter)
All-purpose adhesive (UHU)

Hat brim: Cut a 4cm ($1\frac{1}{2}$in) hole in the centre of the larger black paper circle.

Body: Taking one short edge, roll up the white paper and place through hole in brim: allow to open out so that it fits snugly inside, then glue join.

Push brim up to one end of paper, then glue felt around tube, lower edge level with other end.

Hat: Push brim down to rest on top edge of felt. Glue black paper around top end of tube, above brim. Glue circle on top for crown. Glue band into place.

Scarf: Fold 15cm (6in) ribbon in half lengthways and glue to hold. Fringe cut ends of remaining ribbon, then fold widthways, slightly off-centre. Glue first piece around neck (about 1.5cm ($\frac{1}{2}$in) below brim), joining ends inside fold of second piece, as illustrated.

Face: Glue nose into position, with labels for eyes, as shown.

Buttons: Stick labels down centre front.

Small snowman

Materials:
White cartridge-weight paper: 7 x 23cm ($2\frac{3}{4}$ x 9in)
Stiff black paper: 4cm ($1\frac{1}{2}$in) diameter circle
Medium-weight black paper: 2 x 9cm ($\frac{3}{4}$ x $5\frac{1}{2}$in) and a 2.5cm (1in) diameter circle
White felt: 5 x 9cm (2 x $3\frac{1}{2}$in)
27cm ($10\frac{3}{4}$in) ribbon, 1.5cm ($\frac{1}{2}$in) wide, for hatband and scarf
Small wooden bead for nose (about 5mm diameter)
Tiny black glass beads for eyes
20cm (8in) strong thread or fine cord to hang
All-purpose adhesive (UHU)

Hat brim: Cut a 2.5cm (1in) hole in the centre of the larger black paper circle.

Body: As Large Snowman.

Hat: As Large Snowman – but knot looped thread through centre of crown before gluing into place.

Scarf: Cut 10 and 7cm (4 and $2\frac{3}{4}$in) lengths of ribbon. Fringe cut ends of shorter piece, then fold widthways, slightly off-centre. Glue longer piece around neck (about 1cm ($\frac{3}{8}$in) below brim), joining ends inside fold of second piece, as illustrated.

Face: Glue nose and eyes into position, as shown.

Choirboys and angels

Two more little characters who are equally at home on the table or tree. Very simply constructed from paper, it would be easy to scale them up, for a larger table decoration.

Materials:
Coloured cartridge-weight paper for body: 14cm (5½in) diameter semi-circle
Flesh-coloured cartridge-weight paper for arms
Pressed cotton or papier mâché ball, 2.5cm (1in) diameter, for head
Double-knit yarn for hair
Flesh-coloured poster paint
5.5cm (2¼in) pipe cleaner (or toothpick)
Fibre tip pen for features
Adhesive tape
All-purpose adhesive (UHU)

plus:

Choirboy:
White cartridge-weight paper for surplice: 10cm (4in) diameter semi-circle
Scrap of black paper for hymn-book

Angel:
Gold or silver foil paper for over-gown: 12cm (4¾in) diameter semi-circle
Brass curtain ring, 2cm (¾in) diameter

Body cone: Measure, mark and cut the 14cm (5½in) diameter semi-circle of coloured paper as fig. 1. Curve round into a cone and glue overlap, matching lines A-B.

Surplice or over-gown: Transfer pattern to white paper for choirboy – or to foil paper for angel. Cut slits, then make into cone as before.

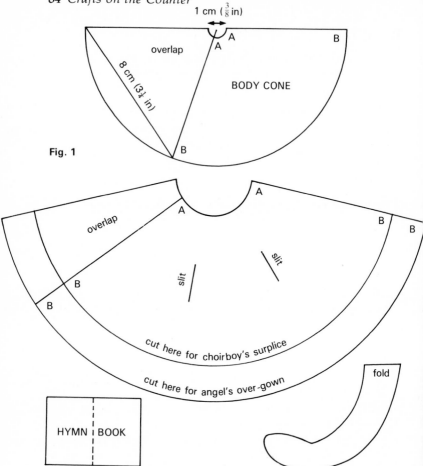

1 cm ($\frac{3}{8}$ in)

overlap

8 cm ($3\frac{1}{4}$ in)

BODY CONE

A A A B B

Fig. 1

overlap

slit slit

cut here for choirboy's surplice

cut here for angel's over-gown

HYMN ┆ BOOK

fold

Arms: Cut in folded paper, then slip through slits so that centre curves round inside back of cone.

Cut choirboy's book, fold along broken line and glue hands into position as illustrated. Glue angel's hands together, as shown.

Fit over body cone. Dab glue under centre *front* of choirboy's surplice and press to body. Dab glue under centre *back* of angel's gown and press to body.

Head: Fit ball on to pipe cleaner or toothpick, and paint. Dry thoroughly.

Choirboy's hair: Wind yarn evenly about five times around a 7cm (2¾in) deep piece of card: slide off carefully and tie loosely with a single strand, or matching thread, 2.5cm (1in) from one end. Cut loops. Glue to top of head, the short end over the forehead and the longer end hanging down at the back.

Wind yarn about six times around an 8cm (3¼in) deep card: slide off and tie the *centre* loosely. Cut loops. Glue across top of head, over first piece, to cover sides.

Trim ends neatly.

Angel's hair: Wind yarn evenly about eight times around a 13cm (5in) deep piece of card: slide off carefully and tie centre loosely with a single strand of matching thread. Cut loops. Glue centre to top of head, then spread out strands to cover sides and back, sticking into place. Trim ends neatly.

Glue curtain ring at back for halo.

Fitting head: Push pipe cleaner, etcetera, down into body. For the choirboy, tape base to inside *front* of cone – for the angel, tape to inside *back* of cone.

Features: Mark in black, following the illustration for guidance.

Note: Add loop as Santa or Snowmen, if for use as tree decoration.

Dotty Father Christmas

It would need very little adaptation to turn the mascot figure in chapter 1 into a bouncy Father Christmas, suitable to hang on the tree or give as a party favour. Or you could make this polka-dot version, which allows for a little padding to emphasise his expansive nature! For extra variety, ring the changes with different colour ribbons. If you don't want to use ribbon, cut the shapes in felt instead (cutting the cap in one piece, as fig. 7).

Materials:

45cm (18in) polka-dot grosgrain ribbon, 2.2cm ($\frac{7}{8}$in) wide
2 pipe cleaners
Pressed cotton or papier mâché ball, 2.5cm (1in) diameter, for head
Cotton wool
2 natural wooden beads, 1cm ($\frac{3}{8}$in) diameter, for hands
2 black wooden beads, 1cm ($\frac{3}{8}$in) diameter, for feet*
1 small pink wooden bead for nose
6cm ($2\frac{3}{8}$in) very narrow ribbon for belt
1cm ($\frac{3}{8}$in) diameter sequin for buckle
Flesh-coloured poster paint
Fibre-tip pen (or black ink) for eyes
All-purpose adhesive (UHU)

Cut pipe cleaners and ribbon as follows:

	Pipe Cleaner	**Ribbon**
Arms:	9cm ($3\frac{1}{2}$in)	7.5cm (3in)
Body:	8cm (3in) (remainder of arms cleaner)	8.5cm ($3\frac{3}{8}$in)
Legs:	10cm (4in) (one piece)	4cm ($1\frac{5}{8}$in) (two pieces)
Cap:	7cm ($2\frac{1}{2}$in) (remainder of legs cleaner)	10cm (4in) (two pieces)

Bend body pipe cleaner in half, and fix legs through bend (fig. 1). Fold each piece of leg ribbon in half lengthways and oversew side edges to form a tube: catch tubes together at top (fig. 2). Fit on figure and catch to bend at

*If you can't find any black beads, colour natural ones with a Tempo permanent marker.

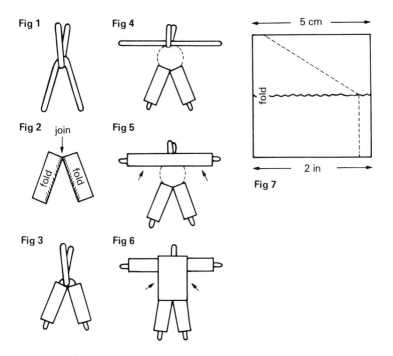

Fig 1   Fig 4

Fig 2   join   Fig 5

Fig 3   Fig 6

5 cm

fold

2 in

Fig 7

base of body (fig. 3).

Wrap a little cotton wool around lower half of body (fig. 4): then push arms cleaner down between body, level with top of padding (fig. 4).

Fold arms ribbon in half widthways, and then lengthways. Snip off folded corner to make a small hole in centre of ribbon. Slip down over body and fold over arms: oversew side edges neatly under each arm (arrows – fig. 5).

Snip a small hole in body ribbon, as arms: then slip over body, folding down over shoulders, and oversewing side edges below arms to about 5mm ($\frac{1}{4}$ in) from cut edge (arrows – fig. 6). Glue narrow ribbon around hips, with sequin on top.

Glue beads on protruding ends of arms and legs. Paint head and, when dry, fix in position.

Glue cotton wool over head, for hair.

Join the two cap strips to make one piece, by placing

right sides together and oversewing one long edge. Open out flat and then fold across join, right side inside. Stitch as indicated by broken lines, fig. 7. Turn to right side (do not trim seam – leave excess inside). Push one end of pipe cleaner into point of cap: catch other end near base of seam. Glue cap into position, then bend point down into shape.

Glue more cotton wool to face for beard. Glue nose to centre of face, and mark dots for eyes.

Shimmering raindrops

A dainty trim for the tree which takes very little time to make, and is ideal for mass-production. These are equally effective in gold or silver.

Materials:
24cm (9¾in) silver or gold ribbon, 3mm (⅛in) wide
  Large pearl bead
  Small silver or gold bead ⎫ or alternative
  Tiny plain glass bead ⎭
Black sewing thread
All-purpose adhesive (UHU)

Mark ribbon with pins, as fig. 1.

Curve shorter end round to form a circle, and glue cut end level with pin (see fig. 2).

Remove pin and push needle through same hole (fig. 3). Thread on small bead, large bead, then tiny bead: thread back through large and small beads, then through ribbon. Secure thread so that tiny bead hangs resting on ribbon, as fig. 4.

Pinch top of ribbon to form tear-drop shape (fig. 5).

Curve centre section of ribbon round and glue to top at each side of fold (x's – fig. 6), marked point level with fold (remove pin).

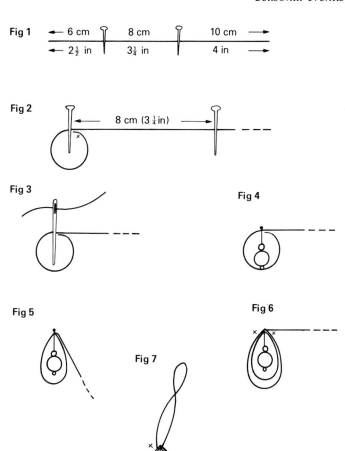

Fig 1   ← 6 cm   8 cm   10 cm →
        ← 2½ in   3¼ in   4 in →

Fig 2   ← 8 cm (3¼ in) →

Fig 3

Fig 4

Fig 5

Fig 6

Fig 7

Curve remainder of ribbon round and glue cut end level with fold (x – fig. 7).

Make a loop of thread at the top to hang (fig. 7).

7 Presentation and Packing
Looking better than the competition

You should never feel the need to apologise for your work. If it isn't good enough, you shouldn't be trying to sell it. And if it *is* good (and as long as you're honest with yourself, you are as reliable a judge of its quality as anyone else) then be proud of it. You owe it to yourself – and that means your craftsmanship – to have pride in what you have created. But no matter how good your work, there is a little extra detail which gives your product that touch of class: presentation.

The appearance of the work itself is most important. First impressions mean everything in business. So, remembering the professional approach, it is vital to set oneself the highest standards – and stick to them right through to the final item of every order. Anything that does not measure up *has* to be rejected! Check for cleanliness: no inadvertent grubby marks or spots of glue . . . and make sure all threads are finished off neatly. Give each item a final 'once-over' before you pack up your goods for delivery: then you will be quite sure in your own mind that there can be no cause for criticism.

We have already noticed the allure of that magic description, 'hand-made', which is proudly boasted by so many people. 'Home-made', 'individually-made' and 'home-produced' are a few more terms used to encourage people to buy. Well, *your* work is all of these things! As it is obviously such a valuable recommendation, why don't *you* exploit it, too!

Attach a label to your product. Give it a name: perhaps

something emotive like, 'Emily-Jane, the lovable rag doll'; or label a cream jug, 'direct from the potter's wheel'; describe a floral setting, 'everlasting flowers – arranged for you'; mention that your 'exclusive lampshades' are 'individually designed'; and really go to town depicting the texture and flavour of your crumbly, melt-in-the-mouth, old-fashioned fudge . . .

You will have caught the drift by now. If you set your imagination to work, you'll become a creative writer in no time! Seriously though, before you dismiss this suggestion as flippant, give a thought to all those evocative television commercials conjuring up memories of golden harvests and farmhouse teas. Would manufacturers waste their advertising budgets stressing such old-fashioned, homely qualities if they didn't help to sell the product? Take advantage of experience within the trade, and emphasise all those commendable qualities which are what your work is all about.

Aside from an emotive description, there are plenty of other ways you can give your work an individual touch: a decorative gift tag; a ribbon bow; a scrap of lace; a sprig of heather or tiny artificial flower; a related accessory (secure a useful wooden spoon to the pocket of an apron – or a pencil to a decoratively covered note-pad). Of course, any of these things will add to the cost of your product. But they will also lift it out of the ordinary, and ensure it is something special – allowing you to ask a higher price for a quality product. This will more than cover your costs, and thus increase your profit.

After these little individual touches, the most obvious way to make your product highly presentable is tasteful packaging. A box or special wrapping will give any item more appeal: the drawback is that specially purchased boxes can involve one in considerable additional expense. If you *can* find an inexpensive source of supply, a cardboard box to fit your product is ideal, because it protects the contents as well as making them look exclusive. But if this means an out-of-proportion increase in overall costs, and your product doesn't actually need the protection of a strong box, try to devise an alternative method of packaging.

When you must have a box, try making your own. This is comparatively easy if you cut the card accurately, and do not need a lid. Cover the outside with colourful gift-wrap, line the inside with greaseproof or tissue paper, then seal the product with cling-film stretched over the top. The contents will be attractively displayed whilst being well protected round the sides and base.

If your product does not need the protection of a box, look for novel packaging ideas in your local stationers or art materials supplier, or the stationery department of a large store. Take advantage of the many practical and attractive packing materials on the market now. Probably the most useful innovation is 'cling-film' – that magic see-through plastic which completely encloses an article and then seals itself on contact. One needs a little practice: it has a habit of being a bit to eager to cling to itself – as you have probably discovered in the kitchen! But once you have come to terms with that hazard, it is an invaluable help in packing and protecting all kinds of things apart from food. Cellophane, too, gives good transparent protection, although it will not stick to itself, and is best fixed with clear Sellotape or Scotch Tape. Coloured Cellophane is very attractive, but is not usually a good idea, because it gives a misleading impression of the colouring of the article it covers.

Many items can be very satisfactorily packaged by giving them a slightly larger card backing, or standing them on a card base, and then surrounding the whole thing with cling-film or Cellophane, sealing at the back or underneath. If the item or items need fixing to the card, there is some marvellous stuff called Blu-tack: a tiny bit will hold the article firmly in place without damaging or marking it. Those shaped foil containers for freezer food can be very useful, too – especially when combined with cling-film or Cellophane.

Polythene bags are the simple answer for many items. Buy them on a roll for economy, and seal the top with Sellotape, Scotch Tape, plastic-covered wire or a tie. Decide where to put your label so that it does not obscure the contents, then write the labels and attach them before filling the bags. Use self-adhesive peel-off labels for this purpose, lettering them neatly (preferably with a rolling-ball pen): if good lettering is not your strong point, enlist the help of a friend whose hand-writing you admire! In some cases, a typewriter will do the job – but this can look rather impersonal and unattractive.

Preserves, chutney, pickles, etcetera must carry your own name, as well as that of the contents, together with your address, the weight and the date when the product was made. For any foodstuffs, check with your retailer first, to make sure you include all the details he requires.

Labelling can become tedious if you have to keep writing out your name and address; it is worse than filling in forms! Consider investing in some of those self-adhesive labels which are printed in either black and white or black on gold. These are not at all expensive and, apart from the enormous saving of time, they add another smartly professional touch to your work. And they are an excellent form of advertising, too. (See page 130).

When the time comes for delivery, make use of any large cardboard cartons that come your way. Keep any in which goods are delivered to you – and ask neighbours to do the same. Failing that, your grocer should have plenty to spare, or you'll probably find a wide choice of useful shapes and sizes waiting to be picked up in any local supermarket. Have an idea of what you need, and then cast an eye over the selection for likely cartons. Apples are usually delivered in very well made boxes, and so are biscuits and cakes: bottles also need strong protection, but beware any leaks, stickiness or oily marks. If you need a very large carton, egg boxes are specially suitable because they have cut-out handles, as do some other large cartons.

Pack your goods carefully into the carton, with plenty of protection. Use tissue paper only when absolutely necessary, because it is expensive: crumpled newspaper is just as satisfactory, as long as it doesn't come into direct contact with anything it might mark. Seal the carton with tape, and label it clearly with the name and address of the recipient, your own name and address, and a description of the contents. Mark it 'delicate' or 'fragile', if this is the case – adding 'with care' to emphasise the point! It is also worth advising 'this way up'. If you are going to carry the carton, remember to tie it firmly with a length of strong string. Make knots which you can undo when you get there: then you can remove the string and retain it for future use. And try to avoid the rush hour.

You can either deliver your invoice with the order, or post it immediately afterwards. If you send it with the goods, it is usually safer to put it in an envelope and tape it to the outside of the carton: if you slip it inside, it may not be noticed amongst the packaging.

Whatever it is you are planning to sell, the chances are that attractive packaging will help it to stand out in the crowd as something rather special. In the second part of this chapter, you can see some simple ways to make this happen. In this case, the packaging is wrapped around tempting goodies from the kitchen to make them even more presentable – but the methods and ideas are basically the same, whatever you plan to put inside.

Gourmet gifts from an old-fashioned kitchen

Adhesive labels are something to be more than grateful for! So are cling-film and polythene bags. Gift-wrap paper covers boxes in a very professional way; rubber bands hold jam jar covers prettily in place – and rolling-ball or fibre-tip pens make labelling easy. Make use of all the helpful aids to efficient packaging which are offered by your neighbourhood stationery shop!

Fancy boxes

Weigh the amount of biscuits, etcetera, you want to pack, then place together fo estimate the required measurements of your box. Use thin white card, and cut with a sharp craft knife and metal-edge rule. Cut the base and two sides in one piece, and the two ends separately, as fig. 1. Score broken lines with a blunt knife. Push each end snug against the base, edge-to-edge: tape together, using clear Sellotape or Scotch Tape. Fold up sides and ends to form box shape, and tape sides to ends at each corner.

Cut gift-wrap paper 2cm ($\frac{3}{4}$in) deeper than box, and add a 2cm ($\frac{3}{4}$in) overlap. Stick smoothly around box, level with top edge. Cut overlapping paper at each corner (fig. 2): stick sides overlap to base, then trim ends overlap at each corner and stick to base also.

Cut a strip of greaseproof paper the same width as the

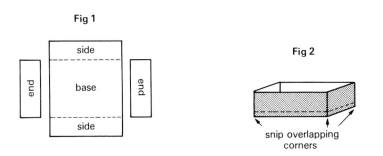

Fig 1

side

end

base

end

side

Fig 2

snip overlapping corners

base, and the length of the base plus the depth of the two ends, plus a 1.5cm ($\frac{1}{2}$in) overlap for each end: trim the two short edges with pinking shears. Tuck inside box, folding pinked overlap neatly over top edge of each end. Cut a similar piece of paper to fit the box in the other direction.

Pack contents in box, then cover smoothly with cling-film, sealing underneath.

Labels may be fixed in position before or after cling-film is applied. Have contents label clearly visible: a small printed label bearing your own name and address can be either included on the main label, or fixed underneath the box.

Potted preserves

To make your jars of jam, jelly or pickle reminiscent of old-fashioned farmhouse tea, give them the mob-cap treatment. Use cuttings from lightweight summer dress fabrics (ask your friends for any odd pieces – you will probably be inundated!). Make a paper pattern about 14cm ($5\frac{1}{2}$in) in diameter, and cut the circles of fabric with pinking shears.

Seal your jars in the usual way, then fix the mob-cap in place with a rubber band, frilling the edge out prettily. Write details of contents on label – and stick a printed label giving your name and address on the back of the jar.

Home-made confectionery

Pack this in small polythene or Cellophane bags (you can buy a tear-off roll of polythene bags), and seal tightly. Use adhesive labels or tie-on tags.

Flat-pack biscuits

Simply cut a piece of card to fit easily inside the lower half of a polythene bag. Arrange biscuits on card, then fold over top of bag and tape neatly at back.

8 Selling yourself
Who to approach – and how to go about it

When you approach a shopkeeper or buyer, you should be confident, without being over-confident! Above all, you should have confidence in your work. But if you have prepared yourself thoroughly beforehand, you should feel confident about your business ability too. Apart from being sure in your own mind that you have a good product, you should know the price you want for it, and give an impression of efficiency and reliability when it comes to discussing supply and delivery. However, don't try to pretend you know it all. It doesn't matter that you are new to the business, and inexperienced: it may even make some people keener to give you a chance!

Even if your knees *do* wobble a bit the first couple of times you try to sell your work to a retailer, remember that he or she can't eat you! And if he or she doesn't buy it, that *doesn't* mean there is anything wrong with it . . . so don't disappear into your shell, hurt and ashamed, never to try again. Unless he has no manners (in which case he is not worth getting upset about, anyway), he will tell you the reason why he feels your work is unsuitable for his trade. It is his job to know his customers, and what they want to buy. Despite your disappointment, pay attention to what he has to say, because any comments he makes can add valuable information to your previous market research. Listen carefully if he offers you any advice: he may suggest some alteration, or a different product which would be more acceptable to the trade, and set you on the road to success.

Everyone knows that the price they get from a shop will

not be the price on the label when they sell it. But not everyone realises just *how* much the shop has to add in order to make a profit – because it is not *all* profit. There is an old saying about 'paying for the carpet'. Well, carpet is expensive these days! And so are rent, rates, heat, light, wages, insurance, VAT, shopfittings. . . . The overheads of a shop must be a constant nightmare. *And* they have to allow for the stock that gets broken, shop-soiled – or just does not sell. It is not surprising if buyers are wary about trying an 'unknown' whose work and reliability are not yet established. So try to bear in mind that the store has its problems, too – and they may well be bigger than yours! Working at home usually means you have fewer additional overheads – and most crafts involve a comparatively low investment of capital on materials and other costs. A sympathetic understanding of the problems on both sides will give you a much more professional approach. This attitude will encourage the shopkeeper or buyer to discuss the matter in a businesslike way, and even if the answer is negative, you may pick up some worthwhile advice.

The retailer will either buy your goods from you and then sell them himself, or, in the case of smaller craft shops, the shopkeeper may sell the item for you, on commission. You will want to bear these alternatives in mind when deciding the price you are going to ask.

It is never a good idea to turn up in a shop or department and ask to see the owner or buyer. You *might* just be lucky, but the chances are that you will have arrived at the worst possible moment, and he won't be able to see you – or if he does, he won't give you his full attention, or feel very friendly towards you! In which case, you will probably have a wasted journey. The best approach is to write for an appointment. If you do not know the name of the person concerned, you *can* write to 'Dear Sir or

Madam' – but it is worth a 'phone call to find out the name of a manager or departmental buyer. Write a brief letter, explaining what you have to sell, and saying that you will telephone to fix a time when it will be convenient for him or her to see you.

Whether they are retailers or individual members of the public, it is essential to be thoroughly businesslike in your dealings with customers – even if *they* are not so efficient! You cannot change other people, if they insist on being woolly-minded: but if *you* are clear-cut and concise, it will avoid the danger of misunderstandings, and build a good professional relationship for the future. Establish a price at the earliest practical stage, so that both you and the buyer know where you stand: there is no point in doing all your sales-talk only to find an item will be too expensive for that particular market. When you have discussed and agreed terms, it is always wise to confirm the arrangement in writing.

One of the surest ways to appear businesslike is to be thoroughly reliable. Once you have a reputation for being utterly dependable, you will find customers coming back for repeat orders, just because they know you are not going to let them down at the crucial moment by failing to deliver on time, or by supplying goods which are not up to the standard expected. If you hit problems – as everyone does, from time to time – try to find a solution, and then contact your customer *immediately*. Explain what has happened. . . . You are having to use a fabric with a different design; there's a world-wide shortage of red crêpe paper, so you'll have to substitute pink roses; a one-day transport strike means you cannot meet the deadline set for delivery; the sudden heatwave is melting the piped butter cream, so could you suggest a frosted icing instead? Once the customer knows your difficulties, it is up to them to accept the alternative or cancel the order. You will nearly always find that people are sympathetic, and appreciate this kind of attention to detail: often they will ask if there is any way they can help. But the important thing is to impress the customer that you are conscientious and on your toes.

Another way to sell your work could be through a stall at a local market or fair. You might get together with some friends and share the cost of hiring a stall. Or if you live in the country, the Women's Institutes run a co-operative market, which sells craftwork as well as cooked food, preserves, fruit, vegetables and plants. You don't have to be a W.I. member to take part in this scheme. Anyone can apply to become a shareholder: 5p gives you life membership, and this allows you to sell your work through the markets. These take place in towns and villages, generally one morning a week (outdoor markets do not usually sell craftwork – for obvious reasons). As a shareholder, you are expected to take a turn helping to serve behind the counter – which gives you an even greater sense of involvement. Goods are reasonably priced, and the markets set their own commission of ten to fifteen per cent, which is deducted before the money is handed over to you.

Naturally, you must conform to the usual high standards set by the W.I., but as long as you maintain a reputation for quality, this is a really excellent way to sell your work, so it is well worth investigating the possibilities. For a list of all the W.I. markets throughout England, Wales and the Channel Islands, send a stamped, addressed envelope to the Markets Department, National Federation of Women's Institutes, 39 Eccleston Street, London SW1W 9NT. When you find your nearest market, go along and have a talk with the controller, taking some samples of whatever you want to offer for sale. The controller will be able to advise you about what is likely to sell, or where to concentrate your efforts. Full information about the W.I.

markets scheme is contained in *The W.I. Market Handbook*, price 85p inclusive, from W.I. Books Limited, at the above address.

Again if you live in a rural area, and are interested in cooking, there might be a farm produce shop in your nearest town. These are very efficiently organised to sell homemade food and drink which is prepared by independent local suppliers. Get an idea of what they stock, then go along and suggest your own speciality: cakes, biscuits, confectionery, preserves, dairy produce or whatever. If they are interested, ask what assistance they provide: often they will supply the appropriate jars for jams, jellies, pickles or chutney, as well as suitable labels. If you build up a good working relationship and are supplying them on a regular basis, they may even help when you want to invest in new equipment.

There are many small gift shops in country districts which specialise in a wide variety of hand-made items by independent craftspeople. The Council for Small Businesses in Rural Areas (CoSIRA) publish an annual list of *Craft Workshops in the English Countryside*. Look for this book at your local library: it may suggest some useful outlets in the area for your type of work.

For that final businesslike note, keep a small diary or engagements book. Make sure you enter all appointments, delivery dates and so on, as well as noting when you ordered materials and when they were promised. And be efficient on the telephone, too. Have a special pad – with a pencil *attached* – on which to jot down orders, contacts, appointments, etcetera. Leave this beside the telephone, so that other members of the family can take messages for you when you are out. Incidentally, don't forget that it's cheaper to make calls after 1 pm!

Initially, it is better to under-estimate your potential, rather than risk taking on more than you can comfortably cope with. It is important that the completion of your first order leaves you wanting to do more – not with nervous exhaustion or a customer upset at having been kept waiting. Try to start off with a comparatively simple design, which does not involve too much work and is easy to mass-produce. The rabbit puppets illustrated opposite page 97 would be an ideal choice – and they have so much lively personality, they should almost sell themselves!

Cuthbert Cabbage and Lucy Lettuce
Action puppets with built-in sales appeal!

Most people enjoy toymaking. But many soft toys are tedious and time-consuming to make – which seriously affects their profit potential. Glove puppets are a happy exception, because the flat body is quickly run up on the sewing machine (especially if using felt), and stuffing-time is cut to a minimum. Puppets are a very popular plaything, too – which means you should find your work easy to sell . . . especially if you invent some amusing characters.

The pair of bunnies illustrated on page 97 is a good example. You could use the basic pattern for a variety of animals – cat, dog, squirrel, bear, panda, lion, tiger – simply changing the ears, face, tail and colouring as appropriate.

The feet give the puppet added personality, and make the toy 'that little bit different'. But for speedier production, they may be omitted: just cut the body front and lower front all in one, in the lighter felt. Similarly, the clothing means you will be spending more time and money on the puppets. However, it does add to their charm, and means you can ask a higher price. Alternatively, the undressed puppet is very attractive if you want to mass-produce as quickly and cheaply as possible.

Materials:
Felt in darker shade: 28cm (11in) square
Felt in lighter shade: 20 x 22cm (8 x 8½in)
Scrap of black felt for features
Heavy Vilene interfacing: 8 x 10cm (3 x 4in)
Double knitting yarn
Lambswool or alternative for tail
Kapok or alternative stuffing
Stiff card
All-purpose adhesive (Copydex)

Note: Oversew edges: use zig-zag on sewing machine.

Cut the back, lower front and gusset once each, and the ear, foot and sole twice each, in darker felt. Cut the front once and the head, paw and ear twice each, in lighter shade. Cut the ear twice more in interfacing, slightly smaller, as broken line on pattern. Cut the sole twice more in card, as broken line.

Feet: Right sides together, join sole and foot at each side between A-B. Gather curve round front of foot between B-B, close to edge: draw up to fit front edge of sole, pinning notches and distributing gathers evenly between. Oversew together and turn to right side.

Pin back edge of foot between A-A to right side of front, as broken line. Slip-stitch neatly into place.

Glue card lightly inside sole.

Lightly stuff feet, then oversew back edge of sole to lower edge of front.

Front: Right sides together, stitch paw pieces to front between C-D. And join lower front to lower edge.

Body: Right sides together, join the back and front, leaving lower edge open. Turn to right side.

Head: Right sides together, join head pieces between E-F.

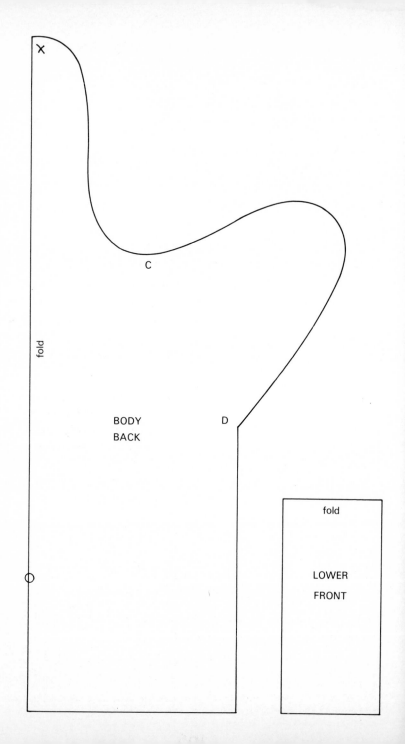

X

fold

C

BODY
BACK

D

fold

LOWER

FRONT

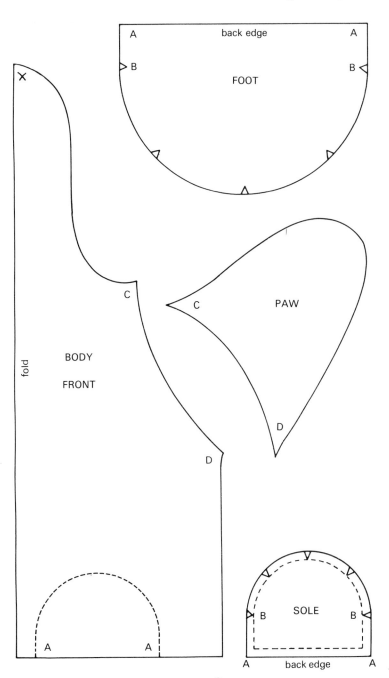

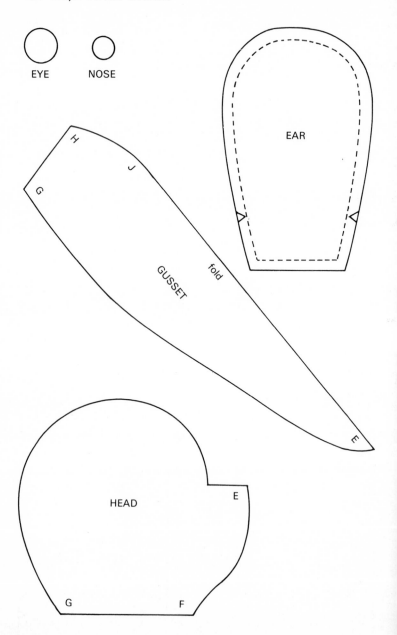

EYE

NOSE

EAR

GUSSET

fold

H

J

G

E

HEAD

E

G

F

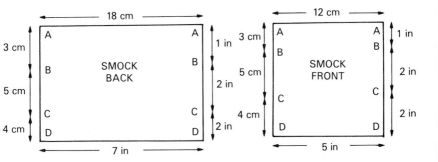

Right sides together, fit point E of gusset very carefully to match seam at point E on head: pin each side of gusset to head between E-G, then stitch – taking special care around nose.

Join gusset between H-J. Gather close to lower edge of head between G-F-G (but *not* across gusset).

Turn head to right side and stuff firmly.

With the index finger inside body, push X up into the head. Pin and stitch lower edge of gusset across back, between G-H-G. Draw up gathers to fit round front of neck, matching centres: pin and stitch.

Ears: Join a light and dark piece, leaving lower edge open. Glue interfacing lightly to darker side. Turn to right side and press.

Pin ears to back of head, halfway down, with about two-thirds of the lower edge overlapping the gusset: slip-stitch firmly into position, across lower edge and up each side as far as notch.

Top-knot: Wind double-knit yarn around four fingers – about ten times. Slip off and catch skein tightly around centre with matching thread. Cut loops.

Fold in half and stitch or stick between ears, as illustrated.

Features: Cut eyes and nose in black felt and glue to face, following the photograph for guidance.

Tail: Roll up a scrap of lambswool and glue to back at O (or make a pom-pon from fluffy white baby wool).

Smock

Materials:

2 pieces lightweight fabric: 12 x 18cm (5 x 7in) and 12cm (5in) square

30cm (12in) lace for neck (about 2cm ($\frac{3}{4}$in) deep)

30cm (12in) lace for hem (optional)

Narrow round elastic

Right sides together, join the two pieces at each side between A-B and C-D. Turn the raw edges back between B-C and hem each side neatly, to form armhole.

Turn top edge under 1.5cm ($\frac{1}{2}$in) and stitch, leaving a channel for elastic. Turn to right side. Stitch lace around neck, top edge of lace level with edge of fabric.

Turn up a narrow hem round lower edge and trim with lace, if liked.

Thread elastic through neck hem, draw up to fit, and knot securely.

Muffler

Fringe the cut ends of a 30cm (12in) length of 2.5cm (1in) wide woven braid. Tie round neck and catch knot securely.

9 Publicity and Promotion
Communication and inspiration

Good publicity is always worth having. But for those who are determined to 'do their own thing', it is essential. If you prefer to sell privately, only producing work which has been specially commissioned, you will need to advertise yourself in a way that will bring your talents to the notice of the kind of people most likely to be potential customers. Take a few lines in the personal or classified column of your local newspaper – and if there is a special advertising paper which is delivered free in your area, try that too. Put a card in a local newsagent's window: take advertising space in the parish magazine: have some cards or handbills printed, photocopied or duplicated, and circulate them to the type of customer you think would be interested in the service you have to offer: private houses if you make soft furnishings – shops if you are a window-dresser – professional firms to supply regular flower arrangements. It is advisable to keep this publicity reasonably local, unless you are very mobile, and prepared to travel distances to visit clients in their own homes or premises.

Ask a local printer (see page 130) to give you a quotation for printing cards. Decide beforehand what you want to say: then he will do a rough layout to show you how it will look. If there is quite a lot you want to say, you will get your message across in more detail on a handbill. You could have this printed, too. Or you could prepare the original yourself and then have it photocopied. In this case, you might incorporate a small line illustration, if you could provide something suitable, to make it look interesting. The main body of the text would probably look best typed (get help from a friend if you're not an experienced typist: it needs to be well set out and clearly typed to look good – an electric typewriter helps). To make your name appear prominently, buy a packet of 'rub-down printing' letters (such as Letraset) from a stationer's: choose an attractive type face with which to spell out your name impressively across the sheet! For either printed or duplicated literature, it might be attractive to use a tinted paper: discuss this with your supplier.

Depending on the nature of your craft, you might get local galleries to exhibit your work – or perhaps the public libraries – and you could advertise discreetly alongside for commissions. Include your telephone number, if possible: it is a great help if interested customers can give you a ring to discuss the matter informally before coming to any firm decision. A local hotel or restaurant might allow you to have a small showcase where you could display examples of your work. Include a clearly set-out card giving your name, address, telephone number, and a brief description of who you are or what you do. If you make jewellery or fashion accessories, you might be able to come to a similar arrangement with a local hairdresser (don't display anything too valuable, though – it might disappear!).

If you enjoy meeting and talking to people, offer to give talks to local women's organisations. They are always keen to get interesting speakers, and if you can demonstrate your skills and chat to the members about your craft, they will welcome the opportunity to have you. They usually pay only expenses, but it is a very good way to get known and recommended. It is always surprising how fast, and how far, word-of-mouth travels.

Another form of 'personal recommendation' is a newspaper editorial. Contact the features editor of your local newspaper: you never know, they might decide to write an article about you and what you do – especially if you can give it an intriguing twist or topical connection. This is always excellent publicity, quite apart from the fact that it costs you nothing!

Two brief warnings. Only in exceptional circumstances should you promote your product by giving away 'free samples'. If people are sufficiently keen on your work, they should buy it: your time is too valuable to waste making things for no return. And beware of doing things for friends, unless they pay the proper going rate. Remember, you're in *business* now!

If you are artistic – do your own thing

Artistic talent takes many different forms, and yours may lie in anything from pottery to pokerwork – cake-decoration to dressmaking. But if you *can* use your special flair to create something very individual which attracts customers, it can be immensely interesting, as well as financially rewarding.

The difference between making in quantity, and creating a once-off design to order, is obvious. It means you cannot cut costs or time by buying in bulk or mass-production. So the customer must expect to pay more than they would for a similar article in a shop. But for you, there is all the creative satisfaction without any sense of monotony. On the other hand, you'll have to find your own customers, instead of letting the shop do it for you – which adds to your time and expense.

For anyone who enjoys meeting people, making things to order can be fun, because it means discussing what they want with each individual client – and then working out the best way to satisfy their requirements. You will soon gain experience in 'handling' the difficult ones: those who don't really know what they want – or those who *do*, and have to be gently persuaded that their ideas are not practical! When people are having something custom-made, they expect special treatment – and this is the way you too should present the service you are offering. Nevertheless, do not allow yourself to be browbeaten! Part of the service you are offering is your artistic judgement, so if a customer tries to tell you how to do your job *and you know it won't work* – you are right to explain in a friendly but firm way that you are afraid he or she will not be satisfied with the finished result, because . . . and then try to explain your reasons. Most people will understand and be ready to listen to your own alternative suggestions: but even if they don't give up their own ideas easily, patient reasoning at this stage is preferable to a disappointed customer later on – because this means disappointment for you, also.

Finding your customers is the most challenging task at the outset. Much depends on the form your talent takes, of course, but in many cases the best way to promote the service you are offering is a small advertisement in the local paper. This ensures that any responses will come from people living in your area – remembering that you will have to make allowances in your quotation for time and money spent travelling to call on the customer. Likewise, if people come to visit you, it will be more convenient if you live reasonably nearby.

Describe your special service as adequately as possible in your advertisement – making it sound as 'individual' as possible – add your telephone number, and wait for enquiries. Answer (and ask) as many questions as you can on the telephone: this saves wasted journeys. Then arrange an appointment to meet any prospective client. The rest is up to you. It might be useful to have one or two examples of your work, if they could help to explain or demonstrate points. Don't forget a notepad and pencil –

and a small sketch block can be quite impressive, even if you think you cannot draw: just a few lines or a diagram, to indicate how you would handle a particular aspect of the design, makes you look and feel all the more creative!

Of all the varied skills which you might be planning to exploit, dressmaking is one of the most popular. For those who enjoy sewing on a small scale, making clothes for babies and children can be less exacting than dressmaking for adults: clients tend to be less critical and easier to fit! Throw in the novelty of a made-to-measure outfit for a favourite doll or soft toy, and you are sure to attract customers.

The toys themselves will usually suggest the type of clothes you can make. Try to give the garments as much character as possible: if you are not using cuttings from the child's fabric, take special care to choose suitable materials and trimmings – and make sure the things fit well. If you can take the toy away with you, all to the good: otherwise, take as many measurements as possible, and try to arrange a fitting mid-way or near the end, at the same time as you fit the child.

Patterns are given here for the various outfits illustrated opposite page 96. The size and shape of dolls and toys differs considerably, of course, but if you compare the measurements of the models in the photograph with those of your 'client', you will see where it is necessary to adapt and adjust in order to make a new pattern that will fit just as snugly.

An individual touch of this kind says so much about you and your work: it is an easy way to build a reputation for yourself as someone rather special. It is very satisfying, too: you find yourself becoming involved with other people's hopes and fantasies, in an area where the personal touch is becoming all too rare, and is therefore greatly appreciated.

The touch of inspiration that says it's yours

A few easy ways to make a favourite toy as smart as its
owner.

Doll's outfit

Felicity-Anne wears a romantic outfit consisting of a
blouse-plus-petticoat (which could be a dress) with a pinafore over-dress on top. The fabric and trimming do a lot of
the work for you: a pretty woven cotton for the blouse-
and-petticoat, lace-edged, and with a ribbon collar
. . . patterned ribbon giving character to the pinafore.
Cutting and sewing are straightforward and quick.

The pattern fits a doll approximately 45cm (18in) tall,
whose vital statistics are:

    Chest: 18cm (7in)
    Waist: 16.5cm ($6\frac{1}{2}$in)
    Hips: 19cm ($7\frac{1}{2}$in)
    Neck to waist: 7.5cm (3in)
    Shoulder to wrist: 12cm ($4\frac{3}{4}$in)
    Waist to floor: 27cm ($10\frac{1}{2}$in)

Blouse-plus-petticoat

Materials:

A piece of woven cotton 35 x 50cm (14 x 18in) for the
    blouse, and a piece 20 x 60cm (8 x 24in) for the
    petticoat
14cm ($5\frac{1}{2}$in) picot edge taffeta ribbon, 1cm ($\frac{3}{8}$in) wide, for
    the collar
1.10cm ($1\frac{1}{4}$yd) lace, 2cm ($\frac{3}{4}$in) deep, for cuffs and hem
60cm (24in) bias binding for neck and cuffs
3 snap fasteners
Narrow round elastic

    Cut the front once and the back and sleeve twice each.
    Right sides together, join front to back pieces along

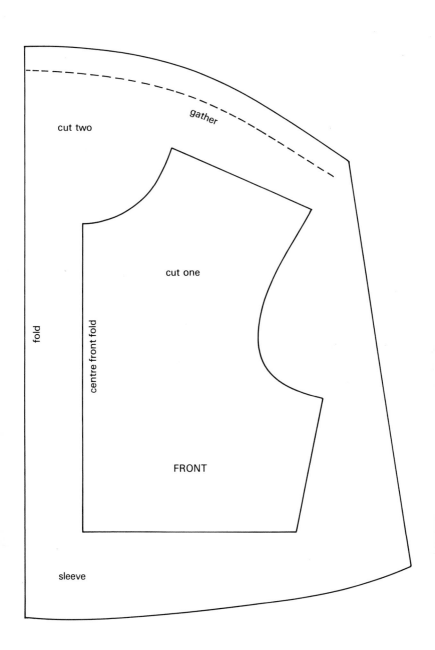

cut two

gather

fold

centre front fold

cut one

FRONT

sleeve

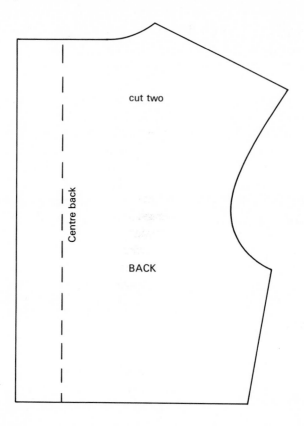

shoulder seams (approximately 5mm or ¼in is allowed for turnings).

Gather round top edge of sleeve. Divide edge into eight equal sections with pins, and mark edge of armhole in the same way. Right sides together, fit top of sleeve into armhole, pinning at marked points and drawing up gathers evenly between: stitch into place.

Join side and sleeve seams.

Stitch bias binding along lower edge of sleeves, turning to wrong side to form a channel for elastic.

Gather top edge of petticoat. Divide into sections, as

sleeve. Right sides together, pin evenly round lower edge of blouse: draw up to fit and stitch into place.

Join centre back seam of skirt, leaving 5cm (2in) open at top.

Turn under and hem centre back edges of blouse and petticoat.

Bind neck, folding centre of binding over raw edge. Stitch ribbon over binding, on right side, turning cut ends under. Stitch snap fasteners to back opening at neck, centre and waist. Turn to right side.

Fit garment on doll (if necessary) and turn up hem. Stitch neatly on wrong side, then trim right side with lace.

Stitch lace round edge of sleeves, then thread elastic through and draw up to fit.

Pinafore over-dress

Materials:
A piece of cotton poplin 20 x 76cm (8 x 30in) for the skirt, and a piece 5 x 4.5cm (2 x $1\frac{3}{4}$in) for the bib
2m ($2\frac{1}{4}$yd) decorative ribbon, 1cm ($\frac{7}{8}$in) wide

Right sides together, join short edges of skirt to form centre back seam, leaving open 5cm (2in) at top: turn under raw edges for back opening and hem. Turn to right side.

Gather top edge of skirt. Mark into equal sections as petticoat, then pin evenly to the centre 18cm (7in) of a 70cm (27in) length of ribbon, wrong side of ribbon to right side of fabric, to form a waistband. Draw up to fit and slip-stitch lower edge of ribbon over gathers. Then stitch an 18cm (7in) length of ribbon neatly over gathers on the wrong side, to back waistband, oversewing top edges of ribbon.

Stitch ribbon along top edge of bib. Then pin a length of ribbon along each side so that the centre forms a shoulder strap loop which will fit over the head and reach to the centre back of the waist: this should measure about 30cm (12in), but check for accuracy by pinning lower edge of bib behind waistband at centre front, and fitting pinafore on doll (knot skirt ties at back of waist, then pass one tie through loop before completing bow, to hold bib in place). Stitch ribbons to sides of bib, and then stitch bib to skirt.

Turn up hem and trim with a band of ribbon, about 2.5cm (1in) above edge.

Bear-size waistcoat and boots

The waistcoat pattern is so simple that it has been scaled down, in order to save space. Just rule a sheet of tracing paper into 2cm ($\frac{3}{4}$in) squares, or place it over graph paper, and draw out the pattern pieces, following the diagram.

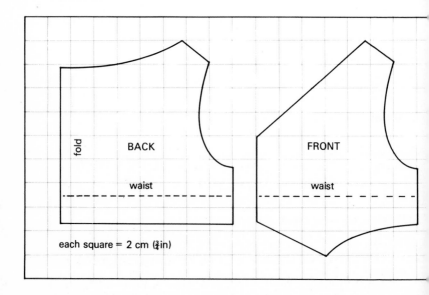

each square = 2 cm ($\frac{3}{4}$in)

This pattern fits a 48cm (19in) high bear, with a 'waist' measurement of 56cm (22in). To adjust it to fit a larger or smaller animal, check these two measurements to see how much they differ from those above, then cut the pattern pieces a little bigger or smaller, accordingly: the total measurement along the broken lines (across the back and two front pieces) should be about 1-2cm ($\frac{3}{8}$-$\frac{3}{4}$in) more than the waist measurement.

To alter the boot patterns, compare the sole against the animal you are fitting: adjust the length and width as necessary. Then adapt the side and front the same amount, so that they are in proportion.

Note: Shiny brass buttons would look very smart down the front of the waistcoat. But dangerous trimmings of this kind should never be used on a toy for a small child – so it's wiser to resist the temptation.

Materials:
Waistcoat:
Dark felt for back: 16 x 32cm ($6\frac{1}{4}$ x $12\frac{1}{2}$in)
Light felt for front: 18 x 30cm ($7\frac{1}{4}$ x $11\frac{1}{2}$in)
1.80m (2yd) rick-rack braid
3 small snap fasteners

Boots:
Dark felt for upper: 14 x 28cm ($5\frac{1}{2}$ x 11in)
Light felt for front: 6 x 11cm ($2\frac{1}{4}$ x $4\frac{1}{2}$in)
Beige felt for sole: 11 x 12cm ($4\frac{1}{4}$ x 5in)
1m (1yd) ribbon, 3mm ($\frac{1}{8}$in) wide
Stiff card for inner soles
All-purpose adhesive (Copydex)

Waistcoat: Cut the back once and front twice.

With right sides together, join the fronts to the back at sides and shoulders, oversewing seams. Turn to right side.

Stitch snap fasteners down centre front. Trim with braid

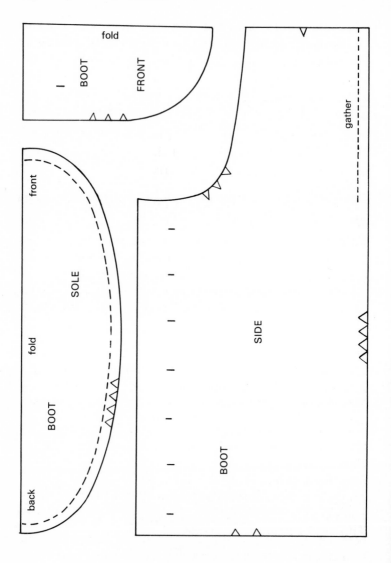

all round visible outer edges, including armholes.

Add 4cm (1½in) strips of braid to indicate pockets, if liked.

Boots: Cut the side four times in dark felt, and the front twice in the lighter shade. Cut the sole twice in beige, and then again slightly smaller in card, as broken line.

With right sides together, join two side pieces at front and back, matching single and double notches. Gather lower edge, as indicated. Turn to right side.

Glue card inner to sole. Mark centre back and front, then pin lower edge of sides around edge of sole (card inside), matching seams at front and back, and easing gathers to fit: oversew neatly all round.

Wrong sides together, pin front to sides, matching notches. Oversew into place.

With small pointed scissors, stab holes at marked points round top of sides and front. Thread 50cm (½yd) ribbon through, and tie at front.

Aussie hat and duffel bag

Make patterns from the diagrams, and then adjust to fit if necessary, following the directions for the waistcoat and shoes. Measuring the brim pattern across the animal's head will give you a clear indication of size.

Materials:
Hat:
Felt: 28cm (11in) square
25cm (9½in) ribbon or braid, 2.5cm (1in) wide

Bag:
Felt: a piece 10 x 20cm (4 x 8in), and a circle, 6cm (2⅜in) in diameter
21cm (8½in) ribbon or braid, 2.5cm (1in) wide
45cm (½in) lacing cord

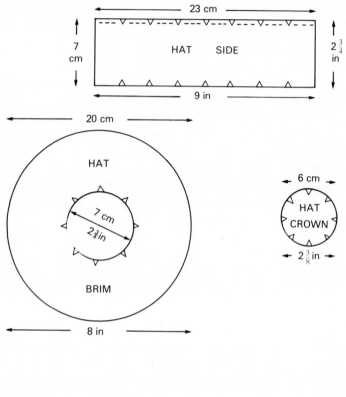

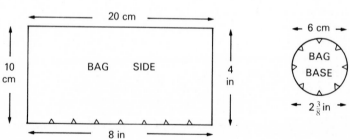

Stiff card
All-purpose adhesive (Copydex)

Hat: Cut the brim, side strip and crown once each.

Right side inside, oversew short edges of side strip to form centre back seam. Divide lower edge into eight equal sections (mark with pins – as notches). Divide inner edge of brim into eight sections also, as notches. Right sides together, pin lower edge of side strip to brim, matching marked points. Oversew securely.

Gather close to top edge of side, as indicated. Then divide into eight, as before. Mark edge of crown in the same way. Right sides together, pin side of hat round edge of crown, easing in gathers to fit: stitch.

Turn to right side and fix band round, before turning up one side and catching into position, as illustrated.

Bag: Cut the side and base once each in felt. Cut the base again, slightly smaller, in card.

Right side inside, oversew short edges of main piece to form side seam. Divide lower edge into eight equal sections (mark with pins – as notches). Divide edge of base into eight sections also, as notches. Right sides together, pin lower edge of side to base, matching marked points. Oversew securely. Turn to right side.

Glue card inside base of bag.

Make holes about 2cm ($\frac{3}{4}$in) below top edge. Thread cord through and join ends.

Trim with ribbon or braid, as illustrated.

10 Advice – help – guidance
Being business-like

Once you start reading the various rules and regulations about going into business, it's easy to be intimidated by all the official language. In fact, the red tape is not nearly so formidable as it sounds – and the smaller your operation, the less you will be affected by things like tax, National Insurance, etc. If you are thinking of going into business seriously, and need advice, look in the telephone directory (or ask the operator) for your local office of The Small Firms Information Service. They will also tell you how you can improve your techiques when it comes to marketing your product. The SFIS has eleven advice centres around England, Scotland and Wales. In Northern Ireland, contact the Department of Commerce in Belfast, who operate a similar service. If you live in the country, more help is offered by the Council for Small Industries in Rural Areas, Queen's House, Fish Row, Salisbury, Wiltshire SP1 1EX.

For a smaller operation, when you need more general advice on any points of law or business which you don't understand, contact your local Citizen's Advice Bureau. They are exceedingly friendly and helpful people, who can usually help you sort out your problems. The address of their headquarters is: The National Association of Citizens' Advice Bureaux, 26 Bedford Square, London WC1B 3HU (Telephone: 01-636 4066).

For information about the W.I. markets scheme, write to the National Federation of Women's Institutes, 39 Eccleston Street, London SW1W 9NT (see page 100).

Accounts: The more business you do, the more complicated your accounts will be, and if you find tax and other official matters getting too much for you, it may be worth seeking the advice of an accountant. But if you keep things on a fairly small scale, your accounts should be quite simple.

The one unbreakable rule is to have a cash book and enter everything up on a daily basis – *as it happens*. If you start off as you mean to go on, it will soon become an automatic habit. And remember to date every item – down to the smallest purchase. Apart from cash coming in and cash going out, you must keep a record of all bank transactions. You will need all this information when you fill in your Income Tax declaration for the Inland Revenue. Keep everything that comes in: orders, invoices, bills, receipts, correspondence, cheque stubs, etc. Have one or more envelope files to put them in, and always file everything in date order.

Invoicing: Prepare an invoice either to accompany the goods, or send it immediately after delivery. This should be efficiently set out, stating your name, address and 'phone number, and the date – followed by a brief, but identifiable, description of the goods and the amount owing. Always keep a copy – and mark this clearly when the bill is paid. Enter payment in your cash book, alongside the out-goings on that particular job.

In some cases – i.e. dressmaking or catering – you may want to charge the customer expenses for materials, ingredients, etc. Make a separate list of all these items, and keep any bills, so that you can attach them to your invoice.

Supplies: Initially, beware of buying in bulk! It is all too easy to be persuaded that you are saving a lot of money by buying a large amount of something at a lower price. Of course, you *will* save money if you are mass-producing an item, and use every scrap: but wait until you have a firm order for a definite quantity before investing a lump sum just to get it at a cheaper rate. At prototype stage, it is safer to pay more for just enough with which to experiment, than to risk having to find storage space for a sackful of a supposedly 'cheap' material which didn't work out. Only when you are *sure* of your order is it wise to 'spend money to save money'.

However, the lower price you would pay for a bulk purchase can be taken into account when costing out your prototype in order to price the finished product – because this will, of course, affect your profit margin.

When you are satisfied that you can safely buy in bulk, see whether you qualify for a trade discount, so that you can take advantage of cash-and-carry stores or wholesale warehouses, if there are any nearby (often a printed card or letterhead will establish you as a trader – or you may need a bank reference). Find out whether they stock any of the items you need in quantity: if so, you can bulk-buy at wholesale prices. Your library should have the *Cash-and-Carry Marketing Directory* which *The Grocer* magazine publishes annually: this will give you a list of such organisations in your area. Or look in the *Yellow Pages.*

Try to avoid letting stocks of an essential item run too low: it can be infuriating to be held up because there is a sudden shortage of flour, kapok or coloured paper. It is a good idea to do a little 'stocktaking' exercise between jobs: then you can re-stock everything you need in one operation, instead of wasting time and money making several trips to replenish dwindling supplies.

Tax: If you earn more than a certain amount, you will have to pay Income Tax. That amount is controlled by whether you have any other income, what allowances you are entitled to, and so on. The Inland Revenue publish a free leaflet entitled *Starting in Business* (IR 28), which you can obtain at your local tax office, or from Somerset

House, London WC2R 1LB. This will give you all the guidance you need about what tax you may have to pay, keeping records, allowances, claiming on expenses, etcetera: it also tells you about VAT and National Insurance.

Ask your local Inspector of Taxes for advice when you set up in business – and also if you have difficulty filling in your Income Tax return. But don't wait until you *need* help. Get in touch with your tax officer and take him into your confidence right at the outset, because his guidance will enable you to start off along the right lines – and avoid problems later. Sorting everything out at the beginning really is good sense, because it can save you worrying unnecessarily.

National Insurance: Self-employed people have to pay Class 2 National Insurance contributions: DHSS leaflet NI 41 gives full details. However, if your gross annual earnings are below a certain amount, you may not be liable to pay National Insurance contributions – although exemption could affect future benefits (this is explained in leaflet NI 27A). It is important to get in touch with your local Social Security officer, explain that you are self-employed and how much you are earning, or expect to earn (in addition to any income you already have), and seek his advice.

The Law: It is essential to check that you are observing any rules and regulations which apply to your particular occupation. There are sometimes restrictions if you plan to use your home as business premises – especially if it could cause annoyance to neighbours in any way. And in certain cases there are definite standards laid down for your work, to which you must conform. These are particularly stringent if you are dealing with food or making toys.

Before preparing any kind of food for sale to the public, you must invite the environmental health officer of your local authority to come and inspect your kitchen. Write him a letter, explaining what you are planning to do, and ask him to make an appointment to call. He will usually turn out to be a friendly gentleman, so if he comes, welcome him with a cup of tea to put him in the right mood before he gets down to work. Apart from judging the quality and freshness of your produce, and the accuracy of your scales if you are selling by weight, he will want to look at preparation surfaces, flooring, your equipment and utensils, facilities for storage, and the general working conditions. He will check on cleanliness and hygiene, washing arrangements, availability of water, waste disposal and maintenance of the premises. If it is necessary to make alterations or additions to meet the requirements, he will advise you how to go about it. The statutory requirements are set out in the Food Hygiene (General) Regulations 1970 (SI 1172), which is available from H.M. Stationery Office, PO Box 569, London SE1 (Telephone: 01-928 1321). If you plan to sell food through the W.I. markets, the statutory regulations are included in their publication, *The W.I. Market Handbook* (see page 101).

Soft toys must be made of non-flammable materials, with the eyes properly sewn in; stuffing should be clean, and there should be no metal parts or wires which might protrude. All toys must conform to the Toys (Safety) Regulations 1974 (SI 1367), available from H.M. Stationery Office (address above). Full information on the legal requirements is contained in two guides, the *Code for Toys and Playthings* (BS 3443) and *Safety of Toys* (BS 5665), both of which are published by the British Standards Institution, 101 Pentonville Road, London N1 9ND.

Contacts: Just as important as the diary mentioned earlier, is your address book. Here you will want to keep a record of everyone with whom you do business, in whatever way. Customers, of course: name, address and telephone number of shop or store, with name of owner, manager or buyer – or perhaps the buyer's secretary, or any other person who has been helpful. List the same details for all your suppliers, adding a reminder note of anything special (good for glass eyes – helpful lady on switchboard – poor range of coloured paper – closed all day Wednesday). Include also your local Tax Office, Citizens' Advice Bureau, library, etc. – always with the name of anyone you have already dealt with. Whenever you come across any useful contact, it's worth entering them in your book for future reference (with some kind of identification tag, to jog your memory). It is much safer than keeping a whole lot of telephone numbers on scraps of paper – which are often meaningless when, some time later, you try to remember who they were. It's quite a good idea to write everything in pencil: then it is easy to rub out and make alterations when firms move, contacts change, and so on. After several years, a much crossed-out address book can be an awful mess!

Here are some useful addresses from my own book:

Recommended stockists

Mail-order suppliers who specialise in materials and equipment for the majority of crafts:

Fred Aldous Limited
The Handicraft Centre, PO Box 135, 37 Lever Street, Manchester M60 1UX
Telephone: 061-236 2477

Dryad Limited
PO Box 38, Northgates, Leicester LE1 9BU

Good quality handicraft materials at reasonable prices:

The John Lewis Partnership (including shells)
London: John Lewis Oxford Street W1
        Peter Jones Sloane Square SW1
        John Lewis Brent Cross
        Jones Brothers Holloway
        Pratts Streatham
Cambridge: Robert Sayle
Edinburgh: John Lewis
Liverpool: George Henry Lee
Milton Keynes: John Lewis
Newcastle-upon-Tyne: Bainbridge
Nottingham: Jessops
Reading: Heelas
Sheffield: Cole Brothers
Southampton: Tyrrell and Green
Southsea: Knight and Lee
Watford: Trewin Brothers
Windsor: Caleys

Ribbons (all those illustrated – including velvet tubing):
Offray Sales office: 31 Carter Walk, Tylers Green,
Bucks. HP10 8ER.

Adhesive Labels: Able-Labels, Steepleprint Limited, Earls
Barton, Northampton NN6 0LS Telephone: (0604)
810781.

Printing and photocopying: Write or telephone: Kall-
Kwik House, Tennyson Road, Hanwell, London W7
1LH (01-840 3222) for the address of your nearest Kall-
Kwik Printing Centre.

Rag Doll (featured in chapter 9): The bears illustrated on page 96 are members of the author's family, and patterns are not available! A pattern may be obtained to make the rag doll (plus a dress, petticoat, pantalettes, pinafore and buttoned boots), price £1.25 inclusive, from Anna Paul Designs, 15 Ledway Drive, Wembley Park, Middx. HA9 9TH.

Adhesives In most cases where an 'all-purpose adhesive' is specified in the listed materials, either Copydex or UHU will do the job equally well: so use whichever one you prefer. However, in use, these two glues are quite different, and sometimes one is easier to use, a little more satisfactory, or more economical, than the other. Where this occurs, I have indicated my first choice for that particular job – although it is not necessary to buy a tube of that glue if you already have the other.

Further Reading

For a great deal of excellent and easy-to-understand advice on the business and legal side of working for yourself, Olga Franklin's *A Practical Guide to Making Money at Home* (Macdonald and Jane's).

For general information on all aspects of going into business, *Earning Money at Home*, published by the Consumers' Association.